Not Alone

Stories Of Living With Depression

Not Alone

Stories Of Living With Depression

Edited by Alise Wright

How To Support The Not Alone Project

At Civitas Press, we believe in the power of social networking to help get the word out. As a reader of this book, we appreciate your voice in helping Alise Wright spread the word about the issue of depression. If you would like to support Alise and help promote this book, please consider the following options:

1. Recommend this book to those in your social network, church, community, work or class;

2. Review the book on Amazon;

3. Share a link to the book on Facebook or Twitter;

4. Give the book to a friend who could help spread the word;

5. Email those in your personal or professional network with information about the book and a link to Amazon;

6. Blog about the book and provide a link to Amazon;

7. Recommend the book to your book club.

Please feel free to contact Alise for interviews, media relations, guest blog posts, and speaking engagements. You can contact her at: alise.d.wright@gmail.com.

Contents

Endorsements

"Stories are powerful. They humanize us, wreak havoc on our prejudices, and bind us together like societal glue. The personal essays in *Not Alone* do all these things. For those of us outside depression, they help us recognize bits of ourselves in an unfamiliar landscape. For those already intimate with depression, these stories can be a lifeline to community, an extended hand in the darkness. They show us no one is alone, and that point is worth celebrating." — **Jason Boyett**, author of *O Me of Little Faith* and the *Pocket Guide* series

"When our journeys take us down dark and unfamiliar paths, we don't need leaders with all the answers; we need friends with open arms. *Not Alone* brings together the voices of many such friends in essays that are alive with wisdom, honesty, humor, and grace. What makes this book so powerful is the diversity of the stories shared within it. No two journeys through depression are exactly the same, and yet no one needs to travel alone. What a joy it is to see such an impressive assemblage of smart, talented, and creative writers speaking words of hope into the world!" — **Rachel Held Evans**, popular blogger and author of *Evolving in Monkey Town*

"A book like this transcends a memoir. These essays make up a quasi-support group, where the reader can share in the experiences of multiple sufferers. Highly recommended for those who want to understand the 'human' element of depression." — **Rob Dobrenski**, Ph.D., Licensed Psychologist and author of *Crazy: Notes on and off the Couch*

Foreword

By Elizabeth Esther

Depression numbs me, buries me alive inside a glass casket—I am screaming but nobody hears and I watch them go about their lives; indeed, I go about my own life encased behind this sound-proof glass, cut off from feeling, sensation, joy. I forget how to smile. I don't remember the last time I laughed. Of course, I cry the tears fill up my casket and threaten to drown me. I wake each morning feeling tired before I even get out of bed. I drag my casket behind me. I pretend to live but I am dead inside.

The worst part is when they tell you it's not real. It's all in your head. You need to pray more. You need to serve more. You need to _____ (fill in the blank). Why won't anyone just stop for a moment and see me? Please. *See* me drowning here. *See* me gasping for breath. *Hear* my silent scream for help. But then again, I am very good at pretending. Perhaps they don't see me because I make it seem like I really am alive. It's all so confusing.

This is Depression. It is confusing and thick. It is a fog of war—a war on your mind, your body. It is tricky and elusive, just when you think maybe you've got a handle on this slippery thing, it gets away from you again. And oh, it is real. So real. This is the first victory: to say it is real. To stop denying it. To accept that while we don't understand everything about it, it *is* real.

And the second victory is to say: it is not my fault. This, sometimes, is the hardest battle to win. But it must be won because otherwise we'll never get to the place where we can seek and accept help. Oddly, this victory is not won by fighting. It is won by surrendering, by simply taking a deep breath and accepting that though we are powerless against this invisible enemy, we are not alone.

This, then, is the reason for this much needed book. I am not alone. You are not alone. We are not alone. I see you in your soundproof glass casket, I hear your cries, and I weep with you. I may not have the cure, but I will be with you. These stories will be with you. These stories are our acts of defiance against Depression, these are messages written from deep within the caskets of Depression. Read them. Hold them close.

And know that you are not alone.

Preface

In December of 2010, as we were wrapping up submissions for *The Practice of Love, Volume One*, a friend of mine suggested I check out a series of blog posts by Alise Wright, one of the contributing writers. She was posting a series of stories on her blog called "Not Alone". As I read through the first few, I was immediately captured by the idea of people openly and honestly sharing their stories about depression. They were not intended to instantly heal anyone, or magically make the depression go away. They were simply intended to share the experience.

Those original posts reminded me of the brilliance of spaces like Alcoholics Anonymous. The ritual of gathering together and telling stories of our brokenness offers it's own healing in ways that doctors and psychiatrists, and ministers can't. There's something deeply penetrating about recognizing we are not alone in our suffering.

As I thought about the idea, I approached Alise about turning those stories into a longer form book. My hope was to elevate Alise's idea into something that could, and no doubt would, find a larger audience. Depression is one of those issues that seems to touch everyone, myself included. How much I would have given at the time to simply sit in the midst of these stories and soak them in. The value of these stories is first recognizing that supreme desire of our hearts: an empathetic connection with another human being, to see that we are not alone.

As with all Community projects, and because of the nature of the content, we've chosen not to edit for language, and in some cases for grammar. We wanted to maintain the distinctive voice and thought process of each writer. Our hope is that in these pages you would begin to share in the experience of what it means to be human. Sometimes it's not pretty. Sometimes it's downright ugly. But in the midst of this suffering, we learn that we can overcome, that we are worth it, and that we can continue.

Much love

Jonathan Brink, Publisher

Awareness

Send.

The email that I'd been sitting on for several weeks was off. For the first time after my second child had been born, I had written out all of the symptoms that I'd been feeling for months. Sadness. Lethargy. Exhaustion. Boredom. Anger.

I knew I was neglecting so many things. My personal hygiene was suffering. I couldn't do simple things like keeping up with the laundry or cleaning up after the previous evening's meal. If my husband mentioned anything about these lapses, I took it very personally, assuming that it was an attack on me, no matter how he said it. If we made a plan to do something and we had to change those plans, I would feel absolutely devastated and completely collapse in a heap of tears. My reactions were in no way proportional to the circumstances.

I couldn't understand it. I loved being a mom. Having children was something that I never knew that I wanted, but when I had my first, I was absolutely hooked. I had a loving husband and two beautiful children. So depression never really entered my mind as a possibility. That was something that "other" people dealt with. I had always been a happy, giggly, silly person. And I was doing exactly what I wanted to do by being a full-time mom to my kids. Everything in my life was about as perfect as it could be.

And more than that, I was a Christian. Growing up, I had been well schooled in the idea that feelings weren't to be trusted. Christians simply experienced joy. No matter what. If I wasn't happy, that wasn't really much of a concern because happiness was a worldly emotion. "Joyful!" was the only acceptable response to the question, "How are you feeling?" And joy wasn't about "feelings" it was about how you *were*.

But clearly something was wrong. I wasn't feeling happy or giggly or silly. I mostly just felt sad. On the occasions that I didn't feel sad, I didn't feel anything. And while I knew that joy wasn't supposed to be about feelings, it was hard to even muster up the ability "be" joyful when happiness seemed like something that I hadn't felt in a long time.

I had read about post-partum depression while I was pregnant, but hadn't really paid much attention to those pieces. I just assumed that was something that people who didn't really want to be a mother dealt with. I had experienced some negative feelings when I was pregnant with my first, but had written those off as being associated with being in a new city with a job that I didn't like and without any close friends or family around to help out.

But without any other excuses this time, I was forced to look at something that felt much more sinister. Something that wasn't to be discussed among decent people, let alone Christians. Something that would mark me as different and diseased.

Depression. Sending that email was the first time that I was willing to recognize that I was dealing with depression.

Admitting that you are experiencing depression can be a terrifying thing. Part of it is simply the disorder itself. Depression can magnify things in your mind and make everything seem like it is significantly larger than it is. However, there are some legitimate fears that can accompany this admission. There are some who will not be able to understand your suffering and will advise you to just get over it. There are some who will shame you for not having enough faith. There are some who will convict you of unconfessed sin. And there are some who will be unable to see you as anything other than the word depression.

All of this can leave you feeling terribly alone.

But there are so many more that will come along beside you and help. People who will give you encouragement without platitudes. People who will help you find the courage you need to seek out a therapist or medication or a new exercise routine. People who will love you with their words and with their deeds.

In this opening section of the book, we will hear from authors who are sharing those first moments of realization that they were dealing with depression. They will share the emotions that are associated with depression itself, but also what it means to come to terms with the reality that what they are experiencing is depression.

Matt shares how depression took the small difficulties that he was facing and made him feel like a failure. Laura tells us about the flashes she saw growing up that hinted at her depression and how she was finally able to see it for what it was. And Crystal shares how, despite being a therapist, it was difficult for her to recognize the symptoms of post-partum depression that she was experiencing.

The common theme that we see in each of these stories is that people often feel shame associated with depression and are afraid to admit that the darkness that surrounds them has a name. They isolate themselves and end up neglecting to get the help that is available to them.

But what we also see is that as people recognize where their hurt stems from, they are able to make the changes that they need to in order to have a life that can be lived not just with joy, but with a full range of emotions.

~ Alise

1

Depression, Hope, And Travis Tritt

By Matt Cannon

Sharing my story of depression is normally as appealing to me as showing people the big toe on my right foot. That particular toe is ugly and likes to stay hidden from view. There are occasions, though, when I have to bring it out in the open for everyone around to see. I guess the same could be said for my bout with despair. It is good and necessary to share what we normally hide from time to time; shared pain is lessened pain.

I'm not sure when my general sadness turned into full-blown depression. That probably isn't an important detail anyway. Both are bad and can become devastating if left unchecked. However, I do know some of the factors that led to my emotional decline and some of the key components that brought me back to a place of peace.

My childhood was fairly calm with very little change and no real reason to feel insecure. Moving only once (when I was two-years-old) and changing churches only once (when I was in the seventh grade) provided me with a false expectation that the rest of my life would be without many major upheavals.

This all changed in 1999 when I was 21-years-old. In April I became the bi-vocational Senior Pastor of East Sunnyview Baptist Church. On May 15th I graduated from the University of Tennessee and on May 17th I began my secular career at a company that builds, sells, finances, and insures mobile homes. In June I bought first house and on July 3rd Kristy and I were married. Looking back, I was far too young and immature for at least two of those things. And when you throw all of those changes together at a guy who had experienced basically zero change until that point, the results aren't going to be the best.

The pressure of all of this began to affect me even more as I saw that what I was doing was not bringing the results that I desired. I tried hard at work only to fall short of my goals month after month. I tried hard at church, but I didn't see the results or growth that I had envisioned. I tried hard at home only to realize that being married is far more difficult than my parents made it look. And the bills—I never realized how hard it was to keep up with them all.

This may not seem like much to some; there were no major illnesses, accidents, or deaths. But it was tremendously difficult for me. I had been used to having success without trying very hard. Good grades, somewhat decent athletic ability, spiritual growth, and a good family—all of these things had come to me quite easily. But when I moved out, got married, got a job, and became a pastor all I did was fail. And fail and fail and fail.

It didn't matter how hard I tried, how much I prayed, or how many tears I cried. I kept on failing. This led me to one of the worst thoughts that people can have about themselves. I began to think of myself as a failure. I know now that a failure is an event, not a person. I didn't know that then. My marriage, job, and church were all having problems and it was all my fault. I began to feel that everyone would be better off if I simply went away.

Making this dark period even darker was the guilt I felt for feeling depressed in the first place. I was a Christian, a pastor even. I was supposed to count my blessings and see how good I had it. I was supposed to pull myself up by my bootstraps and keep going. The problem was that after being down for so long I couldn't do either one.

I kept praying and preaching, hoping and crying. Finally, my emotional pain brought physical pain. My chest began hurting and my left arm began tingling. I was 23 years old and it felt like I was having a heart attack. Kristy made me go to the doctor. The EKG and other heart tests showed that nothing was wrong with my heart.

The doctor then asked me two things that started me on the path out of my dungeon. In the presence of Kristy, he asked me if I felt depressed. I said yes. Then he asked me if I had ever thought about hurting myself. With tears filling my eyes I nodded my head. Kristy immediately began crying—she had no idea. I feel bad that she had to hear it this way, but I am thankful that she found out. It helped save my life, our marriage, and my ministry.

Over the course of the next few months, I got the help that I desperately needed. A good therapist named Butch and good medicine that has a name I can't remember helped. Finding out that I wasn't the only Christian or pastor that struggled with this problem helped, too.

But the real breakthrough happened thanks to Travis Tritt.

My idea to turn the radio on and listen to a local country music station had to be a God thing; at the time I wasn't listening to the radio during my morning commute at all. I spent that time talking to God. That day was different, though. I was frustrated about some things and negative thoughts were beginning to cloud my mind. Out of nowhere I felt an urge to turn the radio on. I scanned through the stations and landed on 107.7, WIVK. That's when I heard Travis Tritt singing these words:

> *"And it's a great day to be alive; I know the sun's still shinin' when I close my eyes. There's some hard times in the neighborhood, but why can't every day be just this good?"*

The song hit me the way that I needed it to at precisely the right time. I don't know the story behind the song, but the words that I heard summarized what I had been hearing from God as I talked to Him day after day. Keep living. Keep going. You'll make it through this difficult time and there will be brighter days ahead. Enjoy each day, each hour, each moment.

This is exactly what I have tried to do. And it has worked fairly well.

It's been a long time since I have went through an extremely dark valley. Yes, I've come perilously close. It is possible that I've been there and not fully realized it. But I have kept going and believing and trusting that God will see me through. So far…so good.

If you are currently battling depression, keep fighting. Trust God. Find a therapist. Talk to your doctor. Be transparent with those you love. Listen to country music. Do whatever it takes to not give up.

The fight is worth it. You are worth it.

And stop trying to hide your pain like it is an ugly big toe. It needs to be shared both for your sake and for the sake of those who are hurting and need to know that they are not alone.

2

Shadows And Light

By Laura Droege

I stood before my dorm room mirror, razor in hand, filled with the urge to run the blade down my arm. The late afternoon light played across the strange features of a person who was not me. Something shifted. In my mind, I saw myself lying in a bloody pool on the floor and heard my roommate's screams when she opened the door. For her sake, I put the razor down and faked normalcy. She never knew.

That was the first time I desired death.

The second time, I stood before a bathroom mirror, a child in my womb and a razor in my hand. The florescent light above drained the color from my face. My eyes were dark, I remember, but nothing else in the mirror bore a resemblance to a human.

After experiences like this, it's hard not to realize that something isn't right. But the true source of my darkness was hidden from me.

The realization came in bursts. They were like camera flashes from a crowd of paparazzi. Individually, they were insignificant. Together, they created a blinding light that revealed the truth: I was not normal. Some unnamable thing inside me was broken. No amount of counseling or pep talks, Bible study or prayer, would force this from my mind.

What was worse was the tabloid headline-like nature of it. People gawked and gossiped or pretended not to notice while walking through their normal lives. Yet they didn't understand what the woman in the photos felt. The woman in the photos didn't always understand, either.

My first memory is standing in my back yard, staring at my house. Inside, grown-ups argued. I didn't understand why. Evening gathered around me, laying the responsibility for the fighting upon my four-year-old heart. Another child might not have noticed the anger hovering in the air or at least not felt responsible for it. But I did and it darkened my mind. The dying sun cast our house's shadow upon the grass. Within that shadow laid the first premonition of my lifelong battle with this darkness.

In eighth grade, I had a crush on a boy. Of course, he was "going with" the most popular girl in our class. Each afternoon, I locked myself in the bathroom and scribbled in my journal. I didn't tell anyone about my bouts of sobbing. "Other teens feel moody," I read in magazines. "You're not going through anything that everyone else isn't going through." I tried to convince myself that this conventional wisdom was true. But I couldn't help but study my classmates' faces and wonder if each of them also locked themselves in a room and cried in the shower and pondered how a whole bottle of medication tasted. I squashed these thoughts.

My uneasy acceptance of this wisdom shattered my senior year. A shadow descended that first weekend of school, when our class went on a retreat in the woods. I paced my cabin. Ten steps from the wall to the fireplace, pivot, ten steps back to the wall. "Are you okay,

Laura?" a friend asked.

Of course I wasn't okay. Of course I answered I was okay. I didn't understand that it was okay to say I wasn't okay. What word could capture this feeling? I didn't have a name for my affliction, not yet.

A flash of understanding came a few months later. Two friends and I were walking out of the mall. Sunshine and clouds mixed in the sky and a cool breeze and mist floated around us. I stretched out my arms, tilting my head back. Raindrops splashed on my skin. So this is what happiness feels like. Then the darkness dropped once more. As I grappled with the contrast between the two feelings, a word emerged in my mind: depression. I am depressed. One-half of my problem was named; the other half was still hidden.

Fall arrived. I went to college. This depression pressed harder on me, and I dealt with the pain by punishing my body. I binged, purged, starved. I sat in Bible class, fantasizing about cutting my arms with razor blades; I sat in science class, jotting down the number of calories I had consumed that day. I didn't have the energy to cry. The depression exhausted me.

For the most part, I've never been someone who is resistant to help and I started counseling. But my counselors didn't seem to understand. One looked at me and said, "You don't look anorexic, so hey, let's give you the Meier Briggs test." (I'm an INFJ, if you really want to know.) The other looked bored when I tried to describe my feelings, and asked questions like, "What would be wrong with eating an ice cream cone?" (Nothing, unless you want to be fat.) My words weren't communicating my problem to them. Were we speaking the same language?

My mind became unsettled. Sleep deprived, stressed out and hyped up on caffeine, my moods began to swing. I fell in love and danced around, proclaiming my everlasting love for a guy I wasn't even attracted to. Two days later, I sat on my dorm room floor, mute, a friend begging me to talk. Then my mood went up again. I fell for the same guy, had the same elation and delusions, sang and danced the same sad song and happy dance as before. We went through this cycle three times before the depression and mania and eating disorder collided, and I had the first of several breakdowns.

Friends tried to help, but they couldn't. Other students talked, I know that. But speculating about tabloid subjects isn't the same as understanding it. Snapping photos isn't the same as having camera flashes blinding your eyes.

Well-meaning doctors threw medications at me. Pills didn't help. In most cases, my mind became more agitated, more depressed.

My theology didn't really help. Convinced that I must have done something horrible to deserve this, I searched for answers. Surely praying the right prayer, doing the right Bible study, believing the right things—surely this would make the shadow vanish. It didn't.

I got married and became pregnant with my first child. Even before the pregnancy test showed two pink lines, the mood swings worsened. The depression intensified. Some days my husband went to work, uncertain if I would be alive when he came home.

This time people didn't talk. Most seemed oblivious, like shoppers ignoring the tabloids as they put groceries on the conveyer belt. By this time, I was wary of sharing my feelings with others. I didn't want a pep talk or well-meaning advice about prayer and Bible reading or (worse) assurance that all pregnant women are moody. This is normal, I read in pregnancy books. "Dreary, cheery, and weary. That's what the three trimesters are like!" one woman chirped.

Really? Had she felt the way I did during her two pregnancies? I eyed the women with a brood of children. If they had felt this same darkness, why had they kept getting pregnant? Why didn't they stop with one child rather than three or five or seven?

At first I tried to express my feelings. But it was like my college experience with counselors; no one understood. At the deepest point of despair, pain killed language. There were no words left. Only the brilliant lights and the painful darkness that characterized my depression were left.

The cameras flashed fast and furious now. I was close to an answer. When it came, it opened my eyes and left me blinded at the same moment.

Christmastime. Twenty-nine weeks pregnant. A pew in a sanctuary filled with worshippers. People passed by my husband and I. "How are you?" they asked.

"Not good," my husband answered. I couldn't speak.

They half-laughed in response as if at a joke fallen flat and walked on. No one asked why. No one offered to pray. As I laid my hand over my belly, my daughter kicking and twisting within my womb, I felt that I had never been so alone in my life.

As the sound of people singing "O Little Town of Bethlehem" rose around me, the lights shifted and the words on the screen blurred into meaningless squiggles. The shadows tightened around me. It was there. It wasn't going to leave. It would never leave. I rushed from the sanctuary.

Two days later, I was diagnosed with Bipolar II. Finally, I thought, finally I know what this is. The diagnosis blazed in my mind, bringing both relief and despair. Medication. Psychiatrists. Stigma. The few friends I confided in gave a quick "I'll pray for you, honey" and dropped me afterward. Was this what my future looked like? I wondered. Why me?

But other flashes of realization have come. As I gradually summoned the courage to reveal my pain to others, I found that I was not alone. As always, there were some who turn their backs or shrug their shoulders. Yet I found many other people living under this same darkness. Some lay prostrate under the weight. A few don't have a name for it. Others shake their fists at the black clouds, demanding an answer from a God who is silent.

Still I kick at this shadow, praying that it dissipates. Praying that my children never feel it curl around them. Praying that there is a reason for God's silence and his seeming unwillingness to use his power to drive this away from me, or to give me a reason why he won't.

Recently, I read a line from an old hymn. "Behind a frowning Providence/He hides a smiling face." The writer, William Cowper, suffered the same burden I, and so many others, do. He, too, found the darkness mysterious and frightening. He tried to commit suicide more than once. His faith helped him but did not take away his burden.

Here's what he and I and others see: A frowning Providence, a God able but unwilling to lift our burden. Our mirrored reflection shows our inability to make the depression disappear. We see clouds and feel shadows.

One day, the mirror will shatter and the clouds will leave and I will see God's smile. That day is beyond my sight, but it's there. I am certain of this, more certain some days than others. For now, I pray. For now, I hope. For now, I wait for that day when I will be free, when I will see God's smile and find myself smiling in return.

3

"Me" Disorder

By Anonymous

Few people really know my story. I usually don't share, and if I talk at all about my past, its in ways that the details aren't as bad as they really were. Perhaps I feel compelled to finally lay all the cards on the table and tell the truth. For all the freedom I've experienced over the years, I've still had the weight of... shame. So, here goes...

I wasn't a victim of child-abuse, or alcoholic parents. I wasn't raised in a home that lacked love or fair discipline. It wasn't perfect, but I had Godly parents and great siblings. I had lots of friends, got good grades. In short I had a great life. My parents were strict, but not overbearing, and they never tried to shelter us from "the big bad world." I became a believer at a young age, and while I was ornery as a kid, I wanted to follow the Lord.

In short, it was my own fault. So I thought.

I started struggling with depression at 16, though I didn't realize it until years later. I felt like something had snapped inside. I was down on myself a lot, and didn't know why – my personality is naturally very sanguine. My mother and I argued often; she couldn't figure out what was wrong, and in truth, I also thought I had no "good reason" to be depressed.

That was the start. I struggled off and on, figuring it was "just me" until it catapulted me into something far worse.

That was when I met "him."

I was 18, he was... older. (Okay, he was 42.) I fell hard. He was attractive, funny, and compassionate-- he fiercely loved his kids, and people were drawn to him. He had been divorced but was recently involved with someone new. But he met me, and according to him, I was everything he'd wanted all his life. He ended it with the other woman.

I felt invincible when I was with him. He wasn't like any of the boys I dated. He was a man. And he filled up every part of me that was empty and lonely. The age difference seemed nonexistent; we were on the same page about practically everything. He "got" me.

I was 19 and in it, one hundred percent, to be with him. The relationship turned sexual very quickly. I had been a virgin until him – I'd always broken up with boys who tried to push sex. I was "too smart" to go down that path, or so I thought. (I'd just never found someone worth the risk, I realized later.)

I told my parents I was seeing him, and they of course tried to shut it down. I ignored them. My dad put the stops on it - for a few weeks anyway. I was able to make my own decisions and they were being unreasonable. They'd come around.

However, in that time, he'd married that other woman.

But he came after me.

When he told me he had gotten married, it was like I hit a wall and the only way I could go was down. I was devastated. Furious. And then I fell apart. Everything seemed to spiral out of control from that point forward. The bottom line is I couldn't cope normally. I sunk into a black hole, tried to stay away from him, and yet couldn't. I was shattered.

The manipulation started. He repeatedly assured me he'd made a mistake and was going to "make it right." Instead, it turned into a full-blown affair. I knew I was sinning, but I couldn't stay away. The word adulteress haunted me repeatedly, but I learned to shut it down.

Shutting down became my MO. I was rejected, so I rejected myself.

I started partying and hooking up with guys to lash out. I let myself be picked up in situations that were not only unwise, but also dangerous. I flaunted myself and told him goodbye repeatedly, but he always came back. He manipulated me countless times. He became an addiction I needed and would do anything to get. People would tell me "you can have any guy you want" and I would date other guys, but he was what I wanted. Needed. I only felt happiness when I was with him; it was a high. While I didn't want to sin I didn't want to feel pain even more. So I kept going.

I was in a mental and emotional prison.

Two years later he got a divorce and we ran away to Vegas.

(I've never been one to do anything half-heartedly.)

It wasn't my plan to run away **with** him-- it was to run away **from** him. I wanted to start over, escape. The past couple of years were rotting me out from the inside. But he was everything to me. I needed him. I felt happy and almost giddy when I was with him, and would do anything to have a few hours before he had to go home to his kids...and her. He insisted she knew he didn't love her, but he still left me. Then the darkness would come – the anger and jealousy. I hated him. I hated her. I hated myself most. I broke my hand on a steering wheel because of that darkness. I ended up living in a vicious cycle of mood swings, having episodes that wildly swung from one side of the emotional pendulum to the other. It was mostly internal; no one ever saw, and though I had a roommate at the time, it was easy to hide. I became an expert at hiding and living behind a facade.

The "episodes" or mood swings could happen within minutes. I instinctively felt something was wrong with me, but I had no idea what it was or how to deal with it. I decided to run away, leave the state. My family knew nothing of the situation and I could never tell them what I was doing. So I lied.

He took it as his final shot and filed the papers for divorce the next day.

In Vegas, my desire to keep cultivating that "high" combined with the devastation of my heart pushed me to continue to lash out - mainly against myself. I partied, I drank, I cheated, and I chain-smoked and starved myself. We ended up living together, which brought me horrible guilt over his children. Two of them had gone to live with their mother when he moved to Vegas. The other two lived with us – they were old enough to know what was going on. Guilt and more guilt. The only thing that kept me sane was dancing. I spent hours in the studio every day to escape.

It wasn't until I thought I was pregnant that I hit bottom. He couldn't get me pregnant... he'd had that detail taken care of after his children were born. My addictions were catching up with me and I was terrified. All the guilt, shame, pain, and weight of my sins came crashing down on me in the two months I waited.

It was shortly after that God yanked me out, literally overnight.

It turned out I wasn't pregnant. And while I was free from the circumstance, I wasn't free emotionally.

Fast forward... God restored me in a relationship that ended up in a beautiful marriage with someone I had known since I was in high school. The "episodes" eased for a while, but got to the point that my new husband was threatening to take me to the hospital. It should've been the happiest point in my life but it wasn't. I had repented of my sins and knew, logically, God had forgiven me... but I hadn't forgiven myself. I had terrible struggles with sexual addiction. I had rebounded from my lifestyle to marriage. Even though he knew the situation I had come out of, I felt guilty and that I somehow tricked him into marrying me. He was the good guy. I was the black sheep. To make matters worse, I was (inwardly) desperately missing... him. My addiction. But that part of my life was over - it had been severed cold turkey.

I loved my husband, but I hated myself. He started recognizing the patterns of the mood swings long before I did- he knew every time I was really "happy" I was going to crash, so he'd try and talk me down from the ledge. That only made the crashes happen faster. It was a dark time. I lived in utter fear... knowledge actually... that I was going to be lucky to someday see my 30th birthday.

It was that fear that propelled me to agree to see a psychologist. He agreed to counsel me if I sought treatment. I did. The psychiatrist said while I had symptoms of bi-polar and manic depression, he didn't prefer to put labels on people because I had "me disorder". He said the point was figuring out what medicine would help control what was going on, chemically, inside my brain. He said no medication would fix my problems; it would merely enable me to be stable so I could **deal** with them. He was right.

I was on an antidepressant for over 6 years and it changed my life. It was the only medication I took, which led him to believe I may not have had bi-polar disorder. Either way, he was right - my problems didn't disappear, but I was stabilized and I could deal with them normally. I went to counseling for a few years, and God worked freedom and redemption into my life. For the first time I could live in my marriage and begin rebuilding my life. But it was a long painful process.

It's been over a year and a half since I've been off the medication. In some ways it's been easy and in others, very difficult. I still have struggles; I still deal with emotional consequences of the life I was living. Some days I have to force myself to make good choices – I wish it was always natural, but it's not. I just keep going, whether I fail or not. That man showed up in my life, out of the blue, and it derailed me. Back to God on my knees I went. And while I don't blame any of my sins on the "disorder" I've had to face how fallible I truly am. The one thing I know is if I'm ever back in that dark place again, I will go back to the doctor. My hope and prayer is that I won't need to. I just take it one day at a time, with faith and hope that He who began a good work in me is continuing to work it out. That He's working the "me" out of me, step by step.

> *"For I am confident of this very thing, that He who began a good work in you will perfect it until the day of Christ Jesus." (Philippians 1:6, NASB)*

4

Horns And Haloes

By David R. Henson

At first, I thought it was the devil, a legion of demons.

Then, I imagined it was God, a divine guide through the transformative valley of the shadow of death.

Finally, after 12 years, I admitted what it was all along — depression.

As many stories of sadness do, it all started with heartbreak, but this was not the typical sort. This was not the fawning, unrequited love of a teenager, nor the loss of that magical first love to another. Those, I could weather.

It was the Bible that broke my heart.

As the son of a preacher, the Bible was stitched into my heart before I could even talk, a birthright in which I had little choice. I wrote my first sermon as a fourth-grader, and few accomplishments felt better than seeing a row of gold stars by my name on Sunday mornings proclaiming that I was, indeed, a daily Bible reader.

By the time I began taking control of my own faith as a teenager, I held few things above question: that God created the Earth in six, literal days, that Jesus died for my sins and that the Bible was inerrant, a divine, alive lamp unto my feet. The Bible became a near-constant companion and source of inspiration for me during high school. The feel and smell of a new Bible, the leather binding still tight, my name imprinted in gold leaf on the cover, thrilled me.

Even without opening the book, I could feel its power reverberating through the cover, trembling sensuously in my fingertips. Each night, I retreated to its pages, mining them for new insights and listening for new revelations. Even on my crummiest of days, it lifted my spirits. It put the most chaotic of worlds to rights. Such was the power of the Word.

But nothing could have prepared me — a popular, athletic, happy-go-lucky teenager — for what would come next. Late one night, sitting cross-legged on my bed, I stared in terrible disbelief at this sacred tome, these words of God that I had treasured all my life. I read, and re-read, the words on the page. My pulse raged. My breath quickened. My faith shattered.

While reading in the Old Testament, I had come across a passage in I Kings in which God — the God of truth in whom there could be no deceit — blessed and took pleasure in the lies of one of God's angels. If the God was truth, and the Bible was inerrantly true, then the specter of divine deceit leveled me.

The irony, at the time, was lost on me: that the inerrant Bible, not the forces of secular humanism, decimated my faith. But because I understood the circumstances of my life exclusively through my evangelical faith, I became convinced that the experience was an attack of a demon. However, the explanation proved more toxic than the experience. Powerless against my loss of faith, I became terrified of my powerlessness against Satan, fearing the possession of my soul by the Holy Spirit would be supplanted, quite against my will, by the possession of a legion of demons.

As an 18-year-old, I became afraid of the dark. My heart thumped nervously each day as the sun dipped below the horizon. I quit sleeping, afraid that letting go of consciousness for fear that a demon would take over. Terror jolted me awake each time my eyelids grew drowsy. I slept with my Bible, clutched to my breast to ward off the evil spirits, the anxiety, the insomnia. For nearly four months, I was lucky to nod off for more than three hours each night, when exhaustion triumphed over my fears. Not even powerful, prescription sedatives helped me to sleep. I quit eating, my appetite shriveling like my faith. I lost interest in my career as a state-champion track athlete. Joy evaporated. And I feared asking for help from those I loved and trusted, because I risked my Christian friends discovering that their sanctimonious friend had lost all faith.

A photograph of me just a few weeks after this episode shows me with dark, tired circles under my eyes, ashen skin and a pinched, forced smile. I look utterly haunted, hunted by my imagination made real by theology.

Eventually, I gave up reading the Bible. I quit believing in demons, Satan and hell, removing the figment onto which I had projected my own despair. But I could not yet admit the protracted months of sadness, listlessness and anxiety for what it clearly was: depression. Rather, in college, I began to understand it as the mystical work of God who had led me into spiritual darkness in order to transform my faith and make me into a more compassionate person.

After about 15 months, the fog of depression began to lift, and I began making friends during my first year of college. The experience had transformed my faith, and I soaked up a variety of theological works. I found myself resonating strongly with the works of Henri Nouwen, who also suffered from severe depression, and discovered a new spiritual home in the Episcopal Church.

I had lost my faith in high school during an episode of depression, which I could not comprehend. In college, however, I made that same experience of depression the experiential bedrock of a new faith I was forming. In C.S. Lewis' *Horse and His Boy*, the main character Shasta is journeying in the dark, unaware of his surroundings, when he hears a terrifying growl. As a result, he turns around and walks in a different direction. Later, when he meets with Aslan, the Christ-figure of the Narnia books, the lion explains to Shasta that the boy was walking toward a steep precipice and the only way the great lion could put the boy back on the right path was to scare him. I clung to this metaphor, as it seemed to represent my own experiences. I walked away from my rigid, literalist faith, from beliefs in inerrancy, personal salvation and other traditional beliefs once dear to me.

From there, I explored the ministry, eventually earning a Master's degree from a theology school and entered the process of ordination in the Episcopal Church. In each instance — graduate school and church ordination — I used my initial experience of depression as the foundational source of my faith narrative. Instead of admitting the reality of the situation, I reinterpreted the experience through the lens of faith, as God's hand guiding me out of a toxic faith and into a healthier, more compassionate one concerned with social justice, forgiveness and loving acceptance of others.

During these 12 years, anxiety and depression bubbled just below the surface: panic attacks here and there, a week of mild or moderate depression, and a seeping sadness that creeps. But I had not had another experience of severe depression, of the kind of emotional anguish that chokes the feeling from life. As a result, my initial experience remained anomalous in my mind, unique, and an experience of God.

But lately, after yet another bout with severe depression, I have felt even this understanding begin to unravel. Recently, I moved with my family from the San Francisco Bay Area to the Deep South, leaving behind friends and place that had not only become a home to me but that had been life-giving as well. Even after I landed a terrific job with the most welcoming people I'd ever met and settled into a wonderful home within our budget, my emotional life continued to bottom out.

Always a morning person, I would wake, unable to find the energy to get up, wishing for death, fantasizing about the taste of a gun barrel. Already a thin person, ten pounds melted away in a matter of weeks, and I would find myself weeping while driving for no reason at all. The only solace I could find were in thoughts of suicide, so I nursed them, developing a twisted hope that if all else failed me, death would not.

I wanted to give up.

I felt as if I had developed an autoimmune disorder of the soul, as if my soul, no longer recognizing itself, had turned and begun attacking itself, like a snake devouring itself from the tail, unable to stop. The soul can be vicious and unrelenting when it is hungry for itself, eating itself from open wounds. Even kind-hearted compliments rang like sour criticisms in my head.

Pessimism mutated into a cruel hopelessness. I still had hopes and dreams, but no longer believed they could ever come true or that I had anything of worth to offer. I felt alone, not just in the world, but also inside my own soul. I felt estranged from myself, an immigrant in my own world. Even in brief moments of happiness, I felt like I was just waiting for that scrim of darkness to descend again.

The fog of despair became so thick I struggled to focus and complete the simplest of tasks at my new job — writing an e-mail or sending a message. I dreaded phone calls, to say nothing of in-person conversations. My marriage grew difficult. I had kept my wife in the dark about my struggles, so all she could see was someone who would get lost in his head, who no longer smiled and who bristled whenever the subject was raised.

After three months of wrestling with suicidal thoughts that had become increasingly worse and more concrete, I, at long last, sought help.

In order to admit my struggles with depression, though, I have had to let go of my faith. I had to admit, finally, that my faith was not based on God, but on an experience of depression — triggered by the loss of my evangelical faith — some 12 years ago. And this is the perniciousness of this sickness: in a little more than a decade, it has infected and colonized everything about me, often without me realizing it.

Everything I have believed and searched for during that time has been an attempt to see divine meaning and involvement in that first depressive episode. I have dedicated my entire adult life to the study of God, only to realize my own understanding of faith was based on a mirage. At first, I thought it was a demonic attack, and later, the rod of a divine shepherd. But what kind of God would do this to person? A bizarre amalgam of love and hate, of creation and destruction, or Shiva married to Christ?

In retrospect, this has been the question that has haunted me and driven me in all my theological pursuits in the past decade. For years, there has been a seething, wounded anger beneath this question, a whispered despair as well as a manic need, because I desperately want God to be somewhere in this experience — for there to be a God at all — even if it is the cruel omnipotence of a God who would subject beloved creations to anguish in order to refine them.

At last, I have found an answer. Any God that would push a soul through the sieve of depression in order to impart compassion is not the kind of God I can believe in anymore. Depression is neither good nor evil, from God or from the devil. It does not take sides. It is ambivalent. And it is my reality.

5

Never Unloved

By Laura E. Crook

Depression is a big, complicated mess that is different for everyone. I don't know how it affects others, so all I can do is tell you how it affected me.

I think that I was, to some degree, depressed as far back as my sophomore year of high school, but it was never "bad" enough for me to do anything about it. I used to think about suicide, not in an "I'm going to do it this weekend" sort of way, but with a slightly unhealthy academic interest. I remember wondering what the headmaster of my school would tell people. I remember wondering whether anyone would say that they saw it coming. But this morbidity passed and it didn't resurface until four years later, during college.

It started slowly. I stayed in my apartment more, and I wrote less. I've always loved to watch television (my collection of TV shows on DVD borders on obsessive), but my TV watching habits became exactly that, a habit. I didn't find joy in it anymore. I spent most of my time in my bed, curled under the covers. I ate less frequently, talked less frequently, and snapped at my roommates more frequently. I didn't sleep more; I actually think I slept less. And I started crying, constantly, at the littlest things. It was like PMS, except 24 hours a day for a week straight.

And then it would stop, and I'd be fine. I'd write a scene of my play and I'd go on an adventure and I'd think that the crying wasn't a big deal, because if I was depressed, wouldn't I feel sad ALL the time? Wouldn't I think about suicide ALL the time? So I didn't do anything. I didn't go to a doctor or talk to my roommates or call my mom, because I was ashamed. Because everyone gets sad, don't they? And life is hard, isn't it? And whenever I tried to explain how I felt, it seemed like I was making a mountain out of a molehill--that I was whining about nothing.

But the bad days were getting really, really bad. There were moments when I couldn't remember what "happy" felt like; moments where I thought that this was it, this was life, and there was no way to get better because this was just who I was. One day, I just had enough. I had been silent, which is how I get when I'm angry and I don't want to talk about it, for days with my roommate and best friend. Suddenly I felt a weight on my heart, telling me to tell her how I was feeling. I went to her and I started crying (of course) and for a brief instant I saw this look on her face, a look that seemed to say "This again?" And I told her I thought I was depressed and that I wanted to talk to someone about anti-depressants.

She hugged me, and held my hand, and we went down to our school's counseling center (located conveniently in our dorm's building) and made an appointment.

That was the beginning. I continued to see my therapist, who gave me what I needed all along: confirmation that what I was feeling wasn't normal. She gave it a name (depression) and that was enough for me to start looking for a way to feel better. After wrestling with my parent's insurance, (which many mental health professionals don't take) I found a general practitioner who put me on some meds. I know many people don't agree with taking medication for depression, and that is entirely your right, but I honestly feel that I needed those little blue and grey pills to help pull me out of the black hole I was in.

And it did. I have good days and bad days, but my good days significantly outweigh the bad and my bad days aren't nearly as awful as they once were. I'm no longer on my medication, which is a personal triumph for me, but I still have to be aware of my moods and I'm constantly on the lookout for warning signs that another depressive episode is beginning.

I remember during my first session, my therapist seemed pleased when I was able to tell her how supportive and loving my family and friends were. She was pleased that I had faith and a higher power to devote my life to, because that meant I had the support of a church. Her response filled me with relief. She never doubted that I could recover from my depressive episode--in her mind, there was no question. She was like a placeholder; she had faith in me until I was healthy enough to have faith in myself.

Saying that my episode was hard is a huge understatement. It was the largest period of suffering in my otherwise blessed life. In a weird way, however, I wouldn't trade it in for the world. My episode taught me a lot about trust and dependence--on my family, on my friends and on God. My episode also gave me awareness--awareness of friends who are going through similar situations. When I notice patterns of depressive behavior in my friends and family, I know now how to approach them with love and sensitivity. One of the most important things my episode taught me is that even when I

was the most unpleasant person to be around, I was never alone and
I was never unloved.

6

Journey Back To Me

By Jamie Habermaas

I had a wonderful childhood with amazing parents who are still together and have been for 33 years. I always had friends and made good grades in school. I accepted Jesus into my life at a very young age and have never known life without Him. But I've also dealt with depression on and off for the past 11+ years.

I married very young and our marriage didn't last very long. After we broke up, I pretty much spiraled out of control. It ended up with me heading downhill very fast. This was my very first encounter with the monster called "Depression". After we divorced, I felt very alone, hopeless and helpless. I felt like nobody knew what I was going through, much less cared. Of course, that wasn't the case but when we start to feel that way, it's easy for Satan to come in and build on that and cause those feelings to grow until we see nothing but the despair. I didn't know what to do with myself and found myself with no direction for my life.

I remember that I was feeling particularly lonely one afternoon. Actually it wasn't just any afternoon. It was May 1, 1999 and I was

20 years old, exactly one month before I turned 21. I felt that I no longer wanted to keep trying to get up and go each day. I felt that who I was wasn't enough. I felt that it would be better for the world if I no longer existed. I felt that I could not go on. So I took 103 pain pills. I remember sitting there and counting them out and crying. I remember hesitating but then just taking them all. I wanted to go to sleep and forget it all. I didn't want to feel that pain anymore. I didn't know where to turn or what to do. I was so lost. I immediately freaked out and ran next door, right at the moment that my neighbor pulled into his driveway. I told him to go get another friend because I needed help. A few minutes later (we live in a very small town), two of my best friends walked in the door. We went to the hospital where I was treated and released to my parents. After that episode, I was in counseling for a little while. I don't remember the doctor or anything he said but apparently I was deemed "better". A few weeks later, I became pregnant.

While the circumstances were definitely not ideal, that baby was my saving grace. He came into my life and it was then that I found what love really means and how big Love is. If I could love that little baby with SO much of me, then how much more did my Heavenly Father love me? I felt like I finally had a purpose. My depression got better and I threw myself into taking care of this little guy. Depression and I didn't meet up again until about five years later.

I remarried and my husband and I got pregnant and had a baby boy at the end of 2004. After I had him, I felt like I didn't quite connect with this baby. Of course I loved him with all my heart but I still felt somewhat disconnected. It wasn't until many years later when I was in therapy that I discovered that I had post-partum depression after being diagnosed by my therapist. It had gone untreated for 3 years.

As women we feel that we should just "suck it up" and take care of everything. The thing we forget is that we need to be on that list as well. We can't forget to take care of ourselves while we're taking care of everything else around us. This depression that I felt mildly after the birth of my baby developed into what was later diagnosed as an early mid-life crisis. My husband and I nearly divorced. We went through a period of nearly two years where we would split up, try to work it out and it was just a cycle of "mess". We finally started going to a Christian therapist that we both trusted. Things had become so bad that I could not stop crying when I met her for an appointment. She finally got me a prescription for an anti-depressant. For me, it was necessary to take the pills to then get to a place where I could work to feel better. Don't be ashamed to get the treatment that you need.

I was on the road back to "me". I finally felt like I knew who I was and what I wanted in this life. I felt on top of the world. My husband and I were better than ever and had worked really hard to get to this better place. I believe that it was those difficulties that helped prepare us for our next trial. In November 2008, I got sick and then was diagnosed with Multiple Sclerosis on January 9, 2009. I never felt down about the diagnosis. I always had a positive attitude. I was so focused on "what can I do to beat this disease" that I didn't think about anything else or what this diagnosis really meant. It didn't really hit me until recently and Depression came back to rear his ugly head. I don't think depression is something that you can ever walk fully away from. But I do think that you need to be very aware of the signs so that you can be prepared to deal with them before they worsen. I can tell that I'm heading into a depressed state when I become so overwhelmed with life that I stop. I withdraw from everything and everyone in my life. I find myself unable to do any "normal" daily activities, other than just surviving each day.

After sharing all this, I want you to know that you are not alone. I've been where you're at and there is hope. There is a light at the end of the dark tunnel that you may be traveling through. I know it's really hard to believe that when you're in the midst of the darkness. Don't be ashamed. There is a way to the other side. Please do not think that you have to go on this journey all alone. People love you and care about you and you deserve better than this. You are worth it.

"My grace is sufficient for you, for my power is made perfect in weakness." 2 Corinthians 12:9

7

Derailed

By Michael Doran

I was officially inaugurated into the infamous ranks of the clinically depressed on March 8th, 2008. On that fateful day a full-fledged panic attack hit me like a train wreck, my first of many to come. Unfortunately, it wasn't until months later that I understood my condition.

My business partner and I were in a meeting with clients and it was my turn to present the construction costs associated with their renovation project. As I began to speak, I froze. My heart raced, the lump in my throat felt as large as a melon and I began to seriously perspire. While I tried to process these physical symptoms, I knew I had to do something so I nervously apologized and made some reference to the effect that I must be experiencing a reaction to some new medication that I started that morning (true statement-false premise).

I was totally embarrassed and at a loss as to what was causing this anxiety. Confusion became my daily companion, as did the anxiety, which resulted in panic attacks nearly every time I interacted with anyone. As I struggled to make sense of what was happening to me I tried my hand at self-diagnosis. I researched my medical symptoms and concluded that I was either suffering from a thyroid problem or was depressed. I went to my family physician and explained everything to him, and gave him my diagnosis. He took blood samples and ran some tests for a thyroid condition. Although he never said it, I believe my physician was honoring my request to check for a thyroid problem, all the while suspecting a different diagnosis.

Because I didn't 'appear' to be depressed like several people I had known in the past who had been, I assumed that I wasn't. Besides, I was emotionally strong. Raised in a single parent home, I began working at fifteen to help pay the bills. Like many, I have endured some difficult circumstances in my life, but have always come out on top, so-to-speak, so why should my current situation be any different? When my doctor sat me down and explained that my symptoms pointed to depression I was disheartened. My mom had been depressed when I was a teen and I recall what a mess she was during this difficult time in her life. Mom had reasons to be depressed which resulted in her 'getting the blues' often. This usually led to detrimental action by her trying to mask or numb the sadness and feelings of helplessness. Therefore, since my symptoms weren't like those of my mother, I had a hard time swallowing my doctor's diagnosis. Nor could I relate my condition with hers because I associated depression with weakness. I was anything but weak, or so I thought.

As I contemplated my predicament, I began to realize that there had been many signs leading up to this first panic attack that I rationalized away or tried to ignore. For well over a year I had gradually become less confident and self-assured. I had become more negative which was totally opposed to my previously optimistic outlook on life. I recall being fearful of things that I previously wasn't afraid of. I became claustrophobic, developed an increased fear of heights, and became super-anxious when there was tension...regardless if it was Hollywood-created or real-life. I couldn't stand too much of the color red, became irritated at noises and disruptions and waiting, especially when associated with driving. For the record, I'll be the first to state that I am not the most patient guy in a car, but when I anticipated a traffic light turning red a mile away, that is a bit over-the edge. I became hyper-focused at every little thing that annoyed me. When I swam for exercise I would even avoid the lane with a drain below it because it disturbed me so much!

I suffered mental blocks, becoming incapable of thinking through a simple thought process. I couldn't remember directions, even if I had literally been to the destination a hundred times. It seemed that my short-term memory was swallowed by something, but I didn't know by what or where to find it. My relationships with family, friends and co-workers suffered as I pulled back. I don't know if others noticed my depression, but they couldn't have missed my decreased interaction with them. There were times when I couldn't get up the nerve to talk with my adult children because I felt so awkward due to my anxiety. Occasionally I even felt this way with my wife, Cheryl, who was my confidante and encourager.

Like Bob Dylan's 1979 album, Slow Train Coming, I was slow to accept and understand all the signs and the effects that my illness actually had upon me. I was depressed and I hated it. I hated admitting it. And I hated associating myself with those that were depressed. It's not that I didn't love them or have sympathy for them; it's just that I couldn't 'be' one of them. What I am explaining is called Pride, with a lot of confusion mixed with it. I know trying to rationalize my symptoms and attempting to hide my depression with others delayed my seeking and finding help. This in itself produced even more anxiety. I loathed being anxious, especially when I could recite scripture passages such as, "Be anxious about nothing..." Shame haunted me like a shadow. (1)

My faith gradually transformed from an intimate relationship with Christ to a daily struggle to communicate with Him. I drifted apart as my symptoms worsened. I questioned just about everything I believed. Yet I still attended my weekly men's bible study, although I didn't want to be there at times. I continued to attend church, but was forced to vacate my teaching and greeting ministries due to my condition. I knew if I gave up spiritual disciplines altogether I would be on rocky ground, but I admit that there were times I was simply going through the motions. As I accepted my depression, with the understanding that the causes were manifold, I began to realize that God was going through these emotions with me. I never felt abandoned by Him, just perplexed. However, I had the nagging feeling that others didn't really understand.

This much I do know; depression is crippling. It is a debilitating illness that robs its victims of the most critical aspects of their lives: objectivity, joy, security and freedom. I have the profoundest respect and empathy for anyone who has become a member of this not-so-elite club. It is not until one walks in the shoes of another do we truly begin to comprehend what they have endured. As I contemplate my mother's state of depression during those years of insecurity and uncertainty, I stand amazed at her resilience. With the support of her children, and by the grace of a loving God, she overcame her depression. I can say the same, adding to the list my lovely wife, children, sisters, and close friends whom helped me by accepting me and my circumstances. Also, I am grateful to my psychologist for effectively treating me and respecting me.

Dedicated To All Who Are Affected by Depression- May You Become Whole.

Michael Doran

(1) Ryan Lefebvre, a Kansas City Royals' broadcaster, wrote a helpful book exposing the feelings of shame associated with depression. It is entitled, *The Shame of Me: One Man's Journey Through Depression and Back* (2009). I highly recommend it.

8

Whirlpools

By Samurai

Where to begin? I have mentioned this before but I will do so again... if for nothing else to help myself work through it.

I have really been struggling with depression lately. I have never been able to "get it". Meaning, I am not able to understand how or why people get depressed. I am even more confused as to why I am getting depressed.

On many levels depression seems like a selfish thing. The mind gets locked on to me/myself/I, all of the things that are not right in my life. Why am I not able to _____? Etc. The causes can be multifaceted. For some it may be the result of choices like a life of drug abuse or crime and other things one dwells on, in others it is a side effect of medication or injury. Some can be chemical, imbalances within the construct of the body's systems. All of them are treatable, and none of them should be ignored.

To tell oneself to just "shake it off", or to advise someone who is experiencing it to just "get over it" is unhelpful at best, and devastating at its worst. Depression is something that is like a whirlpool. The process is slow and almost imperceptible in the beginning, but as it progresses it picks up speed and the spiral gets tighter and tighter as it pulls you down. The longer one does nothing about the predicament the stronger it takes hold and the harder it is to escape... especially without outside assistance.

I am not entirely sure how long I struggled with depression before I finally sought some help. One person said that she had noticed a "cyclical" pattern for as long as two years. For me the "trigger" that pushed it over the edge of manageability was when my beloved went back to work.

I grew up, for the most part, with a single mother who was rarely at home. This left my brother and me alone most of the time to fend for ourselves. As a young man I steeled myself to the task. It was what it was and I didn't really know any better. I did the best I could to do the chores around the house and feed me and my brother (he pitched in some too, it was not all me). I remember learning to do laundry and make mac & cheese, those kinds of things. I don't completely remember what I felt back then, I just remember trying to do what I thought needed to be done around the house and to take care of my brother and myself.

After work my mother would often not come home. She would go to a pub. She even had rules for us about only answering the phone if it rang in a certain pattern, and to never answer the door. This led to me having authority issues with many of the teachers and other adults. I fell further and further behind academically. I finally dropped out of High School halfway through the 12th grade. My mother never asked me why I was at home and not in school. When my beloved rejoined the workforce after almost fifteen years of being a stay at home wife and mother, I began to have an overwhelming sense of abandonment. I felt like I was losing her and there was nothing I could do about it.

In reality, there was nothing my beloved was doing to make me feel this way. As a matter of fact, she bent over backwards to assure me, to comfort me, to let me know that she was indeed my beloved and was not leaving me. For her, this job was in many ways a "life saver". It had renewed her sense of purpose now that our three darlings were older and not needing her around as much. It has been one of the better things to come along for her.

What was hard was I knew all this... and yet I could not change the way my own mind and body were reacting. I would pray (and still do), and I would "preach" to myself these facts, but I just couldn't shake the rampaging thoughts that she was disappointed in me, that she would rather be at work than be home with me. I also suffered from insomnia while these thoughts ran out of control and my body would actually tremble. I knew I was not thinking clearly, and my attempts to talk with my beloved about what I was going through were causing her distress. One of our long time friends reached out to me, but I felt that I did not really have that kind of relationship with him and did not want to reveal that part of me to him. I reached out to another Christian man who I respected, and who was also a licensed therapist. While he felt it better to not counsel me himself since we were friends, he did put me in touch with a Christian therapist. I met with him for several weeks while we discussed my past relationship with my mother (who passed away in 2000) and what I was going through in the present. It helped me put into focus things I was still struggling with from back then and how it was impacting my present. For me, my dose of Celexa has been incredibly helpful with my rounds of depression.

Now, when the grips of the whirlpool begin to try and take hold, with the help of the therapy sessions and the Celexa, it feels like I have a full set of sails to pull me free from the danger. I've also been able to be more proactive by exercising both mind and body, which help me realize the danger long before I am fully engulfed.

9

The World's Oldest Six-Year-Old

By Joy Wilson

I first met Jesus at age four. An average man, he sat in a red chair and watched my grandfather rape me. Jesus looked straight into my eyes, never turning away in shame or disgust, and until I blacked out from pain and suffocation, he spoke into my mind, "You're going to be OK. I'm right here. I'll not leave you, now or ever." Believing him kept me sane.

I was laid for 1st grade – laid open as with a meat cleaver, laid waste as if I was waste. His penis and hands amputated my innocence, almost before I knew I had any. Missing the Precious in himself, he stole mine. Like the stepsister with Cinderella's slipper, he could not squeeze his rage into who I was, so he ruined what he could. My immature body was forced to do adult things I didn't understand, and my six-year-old soul was a Samaritan – stripped, beaten, and left for dead.

I was bribed not to tell with the ultimate threat: "Don't bother telling your mother. She'll believe me, not you." Wanting deliverance that couldn't come, I had to take care of myself by protecting us from discovery, a game he enjoyed and took to the edge. I became a professional liar to shield myself from not being believed by the person who meant the most to me. I couldn't risk Mama's rejection, so my Mission Statement became, "What she doesn't know won't hurt me."

What devastated me the most was I wasn't sure Mama loved me enough to stop the rapes if I told. Mama was June Cleaver and Betty Crocker combined – cleaning and cooking as proof of her love for her family. But she was also a "nice Southern Lady". Her favorite word was "nice" and "fine" was second runner-up. Unpleasant things didn't happen and weren't discussed in our home. You could be sad, but not mad, and sadness had appropriate parameters, like at funerals and for not winning first prize at the county fair.

Depression wasn't "nice", therefore didn't exist. Bad things happened to bad people, which we certainly weren't. Shame in families, like unmarried teenagers getting pregnant, was dusted up by sending them away and explained to your friends with some improbable reason, though everybody knew. Somehow it was OK to know if you didn't talk about it, though people did behind your back. Really shameful things were kept hidden at all cost, because not only was the offender at fault, but so was the family who allowed the disaster to happen.

I knew what my grandfather and I did was wrong. I hated it, yet craved the attention at the same time. When he wasn't hurting me, I was treated to ice cream and special presents, even though it wasn't my birthday. Frequently he would come home from the store with a treat for his "Little Princess". Mama gave treats for good behavior. All "A's" on my report card earned a reward every time. Approval was behavior-based, something that gained respect from your friends over coffee and pie at the kitchen table. Mama was a good Mama if I was good.

I longed with all my heart for Mama to be like Jesus, facing pain without shaming the wounded. I fantasized about her scooping me up in her arms, and attacking my assailant like an angry mama bear, protecting me with her life. But she was a fragile pansy, without even thorns to protect herself.

So I created my own shelters where it was safe to feel my pain. My favorite was to make elaborate tent houses, built with bedspreads and blankets tethered to dining room chairs with encyclopedias. The Holiest of Holies was reached via a long tunnel big enough only for me. I felt safe in this wool and cotton sanctuary where it was OK to cry in despair, watched by Christ-like dolls that didn't turn away. Self-protection was crucial to avoid abandonment.

Besides lying, my strongest defensive weapon required figuring out how best to make my Significant Others pleased with me, and then wear a custom-made persona for each person I loved. I created a closet full of Joys, like Barbie dresses, for them to love. So when there was rejection, IT was abandoned, not me.

Depression ate me alive the day I figured out the truth. The people I wanted to love me unconditionally loved the handcrafted Joys I let them see, which meant they didn't love the real me at all. I kept her hidden, because she was all I had, though in broken shards poking holes in my heart.

As I grew older, my evangelical upbringing ruined my perception of Jesus. No longer was his constant presence sufficient; he had to *do* something to prove his love for me. Dying on the cross was all well and good, but intervention now was what really counted. Whereas earlier I wanted Mama to be like Jesus, I learned that Jesus was like Mama: good behavior earns answered prayers. The most dreadful verse in the Bible was Psalm 66:18: "If I regard wickedness in my heart, the Lord will not hear" (NAS). So that's why he didn't make the rapes stop – there was wickedness in my heart. I did bad things with my relative. I thought bad things. I was bad. I was a thing.

You want someone to love you? Prove it. Do they have conditions about this? Change. But what if I couldn't do what they wanted, no matter how much I tried? I was screwed – "Jesus doesn't love me, this I know." I must not love him, either, because I didn't do what he required, which was way out of my reach. Hell, I couldn't please anybody, not even myself, because I couldn't please anybody. It was all my fault.

The deeper depression pulled me down, the brighter my stage performance: honors student, angelic voice in choir, and award for "Best Poem of the Year." No one read the file full of hopeless, despairing poems in a drawer. No one cared because no one knew. I made damned sure of it. I hid hurt, and played the game I couldn't win.

Depression became my soul mate, and although we don't see each other every day, we've never been divorced.

10

The Baby

By Crystal Clancy

My second child, a girl, was born in November 2005. In Minnesota it is cold and gray that time of year. My son, the firstborn, was, of course, perfect. Well-behaved, compliant, and always happy. My daughter was very much wanted. Don't get me wrong. But shortly after she was born, I found myself not enjoying motherhood as much as I had before. This little package of pink and bows wasn't my dream baby- but a puking, crying, mewling demon. She spent a lot of time in her bouncy seat, watching the world go by while I sat, sullen, on the couch, or playing on the floor with my son.

People came over to visit, very excited about the baby. My friends commented that I didn't seem like myself. Some even expressed concern for me, saying that I didn't "seem right." Was I OK? "I'm fine," I would reply. Because I was. I had to be. That was my job.

One Thursday, the baby woke up for a middle-of-the-night feeding, and I went to her, rocked her, fed her, and dozed in the chair. I went to lay her back down, praying that tonight would be the night that she actually went back to sleep. Kneeling next to her crib, with my arm through the slats as her pacifier popped out of her little mouth. I would put it back in, and she would spit it out. And so the cycle continued, for an hour. I was screaming on the inside, "PLEASE go back to sleep. PLEASE stop spitting out the pacifier. PLEASE stop kicking your little legs, and squirming. Just please." But she didn't, until finally, I took the pacifier and jammed it hard into her face. I had visions of taping it on with duct tape.

Finally, exhausted and in tears, I recognized that this wasn't OK. Moms shouldn't be pushing on their baby's face really hard. Moms shouldn't be picturing taping duct tape over a tiny mouth. "You're just tired," I told myself, and got up and asked my husband to relieve me because I could not take another morning like this. Another morning of being awake since 4 am trying to get the baby to go back to sleep. Thankfully, my wonderful husband popped right up and took care of her so I could go back to bed.

The following Monday, after another day of not being able to get her to nap, I was standing over her crib doing the pacifier routine, and she was finally dozing off. I knelt, or maybe more appropriately fell, on the floor in exhaustion and in my mind worked out a scheme to take my son and leave the house, my daughter sleeping safely in her crib. My husband would be home from work in an hour- she would be fine there. I envisioned packing my bags and checking into a hotel with my son, and staying there. A week, two weeks, six months—whatever it took. I knew that my daughter would be in good hands, my husband an amazing father, and that if I could just get away and be alone with my son, everything would be fine.

I talked myself out of leaving, somehow, and my husband came home and found me in tears on the living room floor. "I just don't remember it being this hard!" I sobbed. "It wasn't," he said. That was all I needed to hear. I needed validation for the many people who had told me that babies cry, or that she just had gas, or I was just tired. I needed him to remind me of the reality: that I was a good mom and that I did do a better job the first time around. I did enjoy having a baby, in the past.

Within the next couple of weeks, we found out that our little girl had acid reflux and milk protein intolerance. Oh- that's what caused the projectile vomiting and painful crying every time she ate. That is why she only pooped every five days, and when she did it was like she was giving birth. That is why I was a total wreck, and got no joy from being around her at all.

I had heard about postpartum depression before, but hadn't known anyone who had struggled with it. Well, at least nobody who ever opened up about it. It's shameful to admit that I didn't really want to take care of the baby, that I was sad all of the time, that I counted the minutes until my husband got home so that I could get a break. It was frightening to admit that I had visions of hurting the baby or walking away from her, knowing in my head that is terrifying and something I would NEVER do. Moms shouldn't feel or think this way. Moms should be excited and happy and cooing over their little bundle of joy. And when they are covered head to toe with vomit, a good mom will go change clothes with a smile, even if it is has been the third clothing change of the day. Right?

I wish I could say that at first it was a relief to realize that I was "just depressed" but that's not true. I was actually even more embarrassed to admit it at the time because I am a therapist. So a double stigma— therapists should be able to just fix themselves, right? I should have noticed and diagnosed myself sooner. Double fail.

I was able to recover. My daughter's medical issues were treated and she became a completely different baby. Getting validation about her issues and about how my feelings were attributable to depression helped me accept it and turn things around. As far as my career, I now dedicate a decent chunk of my time to supporting women (and their partners) in the postpartum period. My goal is to help women not suffer in silence- to know that asking for help, and admitting that you are not enjoying motherhood is not a sign of weakness. You are not a horrible person (or wife or mother) for feeling the way that you do. That having a baby that has medical issues or cries a lot is a risk factor for postpartum depression, not something that you should shame yourself for not enjoying.

Acceptance

When you accept something, you are saying that you are willing to have it as a part of your life.

Which is why it's often hard to accept that you have depression.

The first time I took medication to help deal with depression I was absolutely terrified. Taking meds meant that I was officially crazy. I knew that my brain wasn't working right and I couldn't think straight enough for any kind of therapy to work, but to actually take a medication for depression? This was moving beyond simply admitting that I was depressed, this was saying that it was serious and that it was interfering with my life in a profound enough manner that I needed medical attention. It wasn't merely a phase; it was a part of me.

I am so thankful for people in my life who were willing to be honest with me when I was going through an obvious depression. They told me, lovingly and with my best interest at heart, that I wasn't well and that I needed to see someone. There was no shame or guilt attached to these recommendations, they were simply reminding me that being depressed wasn't normal and that I could get help for it. Their encouragement was instrumental in my ability to take the first steps toward accepting my depression.

But going beyond mere recognition into acceptance is tricky. There can be a number of things working against your ability to simply recognize the symptoms as depression. But once you've seen it for what it is, applying that label to yourself can be very difficult. No one likes labels and this one in particular can carry with it some negative connotations. Lazy. Sad. Selfish. Reclusive. Allowing depression to be attached to your life can feel like it has nothing but adverse consequences. But it can have positive benefits as well.

Accepting that I had depression meant that it was something that was a part of my life, but it also meant that it was something that I could address. I didn't have to let it rule me. Certainly there would be some who would suggest that accepting that you have depression gives power to it, but this has not been my experience. I have found that by accepting depression, I am taking control. Yes, it is a part of my makeup, but now it can be reduce to a part, rather than allowing it to reach its fingers into every section of my life. By accepting it, I also could seek out the tools necessary to move beyond it.

Acceptance also meant that I was a part of a community. Even though depression is tremendously common, when you're experiencing the symptoms without the support of others, you can feel lonely. When I accepted that I was depressed and started talking about it, I found that there were others who were going through the same thing. We were able to share stories and experience healing through that. If I had not been honest about my struggle, I would have continued to suffer alone, but by being honest, I connected with others who were experiencing the same thing and we were able to encourage one another.

Acceptance means different things for different people. For Joy, acceptance meant stepping back from the demands of raising a special needs child and allowing herself to forgive herself of some of the negative thoughts that she had. Brooke found that she needed to face childhood abuse and take time from leading worship at her church to come to grips with the depression that held her. Jake found that he needed to embrace his depression so that he was able to begin the process of overcoming it. Kristin lived with depression so long that it became her "normal" and it took the words of a friend to recognize that it didn't have to be.

The stories in this section address what it has meant for the writers to accept depression in their lives. This is not to be confused with resignation. Often people are resigned when they deal with depression without recognizing it for what it is. Instead, these authors have shown that accepting their depression has allowed them to live life more fully.

~ Alise

11

Depression's Dreaded Sidekick

By Joy Bennett

"God, I can't do this. Please take her before I screw her up."

I was sobbing as I huddled on the floor, back wedged into the corner of my parents' office. I was numb from exhaustion, almost too tired to blink. I had carried her downstairs so that she wouldn't wake anyone else up.

My 5-year-old daughter lay in the middle of the floor, kicking her legs, rocking on her back, rolling from side to side, and yelping happily. Wide-awake. At 2am.

So many nights were like this. It never failed. In what felt like mere seconds after I fell asleep, I'd hear her start making her happy noises, loud and persistent happy noises. I'd lie in a state of half-sleep, begging God for her to go back to sleep so I wouldn't have to get up. Most of the time, she'd ramp up the whining and the volume; irritated that no one else was up partying with her. I'd drag my weary cranky body out of bed to make sure she wasn't in a bad position or laying in a puddle of vomit or bleeding out her nose, and plead with her to be quiet and go back to sleep.

Most nights I was numb, sprinkled with frustration. But some nights I was angry and bitter. Those nights my words and my tone were harsh and impatient, my touch rough and gruff.

A few nights I totally went off the deep end. You see, sleep-deprivation is a special form of crazy making.

Looking back on it, I understand (though of course I do not justify or excuse) how parents can get to the point where they would shake a baby. The nights that I lost control, I felt cornered... miserable... trapped... incapable of doing anything to make the situation one tiny bit better... desperate. I couldn't think clearly anymore – all I knew was that only one thing lay between me and the sleep without which I could not function: this person carrying on in front of me. Remembering never fails to bring tears and an almost-unbearable guilt.

I endured years of nights like this and days thick as mud and heavy as an 80-lb pack. I blamed it on fatigue since I never slept through the night. Now I know that this chronic exhaustion cloaked years of depression.

I didn't think it was depression because it ebbed and flowed. I thought someone with depression never had good days, didn't experience the ups and downs that I was experiencing.

I was wrong.

My daughter's needs were significant. I didn't let myself step back and evaluate my own needs -- I didn't have a spare moment or brain cell or ounce of energy for that.

Very few people talk about the grief that parents of children with special needs experience. It is a cyclical thing, recurring every time their child experiences a setback or another child their age reaches a major milestone. Raising a child with special needs changes your life in countless ways. A simple trip to the grocery store is no longer simple. Priorities invert. Death lurks in your mind's corners, haunting every step.

Sometimes, death raises its ugly head in other ways. I had some desperate days, in addition to the desperate nights. Some days, it all became too much and I'd find myself sobbing and begging God to end it. I lived in fear that I would make a life-altering mistake. I lived in guilt over the fact that I could actually verbalize that I wished it over. I lived in dread of the day when it actually *was* over.

The weeks after she died, all those desperate moments when I begged him to take her slammed into me like a wrecking ball. Had I somehow wished this on us? On her? Was this my fault? Thus began the rapid downward spiral.

Today, I've made peace with the circumstances surrounding her death. I can look back and see more clearly the road I was on. I struggled through depression for ten years before finding the help that I needed because I didn't recognize it for what it was, I was too proud to ask for help, and I heard from certain parts of the Christian community that it was a cop-out to take meds. I was told that if I just trusted God enough, prayed hard enough, and repeated the same things over enough times, I would fix myself and it would go away.

I had to hit rock bottom before I started looking for help. I am in a better place now, empowered with more experience and more understanding, but it is still a struggle. I have observed how physical things like sleep, food choices, hormones, illness, exercise or lack of activity, and the seasons affect me both positively and negatively. I have also observed how relationship stresses can worsen depression, which then can worsen the stress on the relationship.

I have also learned how medication can help. Some people use it like a cast on a broken bone – it helps them get stable while they work to heal and resolve the issues that triggered or feed their depression. Eventually, they grow strong enough to ditch the cast. Others use medication like I use arch supports – they need something to support a permanently weak area and to prevent further or worse injury. The only way to tell which kind of person you are is with the help of a good physician and a good counselor who can help guide you through.

I am better now for many reasons. I sleep more consistently, I eat better foods, I am finally able to exercise regularly, and many of the questions about faith are more settled for me. But the dark still catches up to me regularly. And when it does, it brings its buddies anger and guilt, whispering half-truths about past sins, present battles, and the future unknown.

During those dark days, I feel like I'm in a cave, trying to climb straight up a rock to the sunlight, clinging to the barest of grips. I dig a toe into *"For there is now no condemnation for those who are in Christ Jesus."* Fingers claw at *"Now faith is confidence in what we hope for and assurance about what we do not see"* and *"In him we have redemption through his blood, the forgiveness of sins, in accordance with the riches of God's grace that he lavished on us."* I cling to the hope that just like every other time, this will pass and I'll feel better again soon.

Sometimes all I can do is hang on to those until the dark recedes and my head clears. Then I remember that my daughter is whole now, and that neither my God nor my daughter holds these things against me any longer. I remember that Jesus moved *toward* Thomas when he expressed his need to *see.* And I know that God loves me in the midst of the dark and in the midst of my worst moments. I burn those truths into my heart for the next time I find myself clinging to the rock in a dark hole.

12

The Boy With The Thorn In His Side

By Travis Mamone

The first time I knew something was wrong with me was in elementary school. I would often get upset at the smallest thing, from accidentally spilling something to getting an answer wrong. When I got upset I would smack myself in the head, cry, and scream. One time I got so upset that the principal had to be called into to calm me down. My classmates got a kick out of it, so they would often provoke me by calling me names. I tried to ignore them, but in the end they would always win.

Finally one day in sixth grade I had enough of it. I tried to kill myself by jumping off the monkey bars at recess. Obviously I wasn't very successful, but when the school called my mom, she knew I needed help. That's when I went to my first therapist. We saw each other for about six months, and we made some progress, but by the time I was in high school I was back in therapy again.

It was also in high school that I discovered cutting. When I first started, I didn't know anyone else did it; I just wanted to see how far I could push the blade into my skin. It felt like all the pain I bottled up inside could escape through my cuts. I knew it was bad, but it was the only thing that gave me quick relief. It was the only thing that felt real.

Then when I was 17 a girlfriend led me to Christ. Before that I had always been skeptical of organized religion, thinking that it was just a way to control people. I was surprised to hear that God was not the far-right-winged tyrant that I thought He was; He was calling me to be His son. As I read the Bible I realized that Jesus came not for the people who had it all together, but for the hurt, the lonely, and the depressed. People like me. So I became a Christian, and that's when the healing began. I learned how to forgive the people who wrong me, and how to rely on God.

But the depression attacks did not stop.

For me, depression attacks always start as tiny snowballs and end with an avalanche. It starts innocently enough with the tiniest little mishap. It could be an argument with some one on the Internet, or a reoccurring problem at work, or something else. Whatever it is, I can't just let it go. I think about it all day long. I try to distract myself with other things—music, work, a funny movie, etc.—but no matter what I do, I just can't stop thinking about what happened. My day was going just find until that mishap, and now my whole day is shot to hell. This is when the snowball picks up the first layer of snow while rolling down the hill: Anger.

I try not to let it bother me. After all, why should a tiny little mishap ruin my entire day? Certainly I have better things to worry about, right? But try as I may, I just simply cannot forget about what had just happened. So I replay the incident over and over again in my head as my anger grows more and more. It's no longer a tiny little mishap; it's now an insult against my very character. How dare they! Everything was going just fine until that incident happened. Now everything is ruined! A hex on them all! By this time, though, another layer has formed on the growing snowball: Guilt.

In the midst of my brewing anger, I suddenly realize, "Wait a minute. Aren't I supposed to be Mr. Nonviolent-Love-Everyone-Christian-Boy? Why am I still harboring these feelings?" But I don't repent; it's not that kind of guilt. Instead, I crawl inside of a Budweiser bottle and drown myself in alcohol. The more I drink, the more the voices in my head prove that I'm a failure, so I drink some more. Eventually I've absorbed enough alcohol for the snowball to add on another layer: Self-Destruction.

Everything is crumbling around me. Visions of violence and destruction fill my head day and night. I imagine blood splattering the walls all around me. I feel like I need to do something drastic to silence the screaming demons in my head. Maybe I'll smash a TV. Or maybe I'll whip out a pistol and start shooting into the sky. Or maybe I'll stick the pistol in my mouth. In the end, though, I go back to my old trusty friend the razor. As I stick the blade into my skin, I can feel the demons escape through the fresh cut in my arm. A few strokes later, and then it's over. The voices stop. Everything is quite again. The snowball finally crashed.

I beg God for forgiveness and promise not to do it again. I tell my therapist that I made a mistake, but I'm really serious about cleaning up my act. A few months go by and things are okay. No real worries. I use all the techniques my therapist taught me. Things are under control. But secretly I know that it won't be long before another tiny little snowball will start falling down the mountain.

A few years ago while I was driving to work, I thought about a then-recent depression spell I had. Why do I still have these relapses?

Why, after everything I've learned, do I keep going through these cycles of breaking down and repenting? The Bible mentions Jesus driving demons out of a man who hid in caves and cut himself with rocks. When would all my demons finally be gone?

It's in these moments of questioning that I remember the thorn in Paul's flesh (2 Corinthians 12:7). Although the Bible never says what exactly that thorn was, Paul writes about he begged the Lord three times to remove it. But then the Lord responds, "My grace is sufficient for you, for my power is made perfect in weakness" (verse 9).

I can't imagine how my weakness and hang-ups can possibly give glory to God. When people look at me, I want them to see a strong man, a man whose life has been changed by God. More often, however, people see my failures and moments of weakness when I let this depression drag me down. What kind of testimony is that supposed to give?

Or maybe that's exactly the kind of testimony I'm supposed to give. If I had the strength to battle my proverbial demons on my own, I would have never given my life to Jesus in the first place. But the truth is I'm not. I tried to do it on my own, but just fell back into the same cycle of depression and getting better and falling back again. Then when I became a Christian I realized that I didn't have to battle it alone. In fact, the battle is not even mine to begin with; it's God's. There are moments when it seems as if all is lost, and the darkness is completely taking over. But then there always ends up being something to keep me going. It could be a Bible verse, a memory of being blessed, or a gut feeling that everything's going to be okay. God's mercy always shines through the darkness.

There is a particular Bible verse that comes to mind: "Praise be to the God and Father of our Lord Jesus Christ, the Father of compassion and the God of all comfort, who comforts us in all our troubles, so that we can comfort those in trouble with the comfort we ourselves have received from God" (2 Corinthians 1:3-4). Maybe there's some one out there right now, huddled up in his or her room, wondering when the darkness will end. Maybe this person is waiting to hear a story such as mine, a story that will make him or her realize, "Hey, I'm not alone!"

For years I've denied having a thorn in my flesh. Now not only do I acknowledge it, but I know that I have to care for it when I feel the slightest sting. Throughout my life I've begged God to remove my thorn. But now I know that it serves a purpose here on earth, although I maybe not see it at first. And when the Resurrection happens and I'm giving a brand new body, I'll finally feel the joy of no longing having a thorn in my flesh.

13

Depression Defined

by Misty Chaffins

Depression:

- a mental state characterized by a pessimistic sense of inadequacy and a despondent lack of activity

- sad feelings of gloom and inadequacy

- depressive disorder: a state of depression and anhedonia (an inability to experience pleasure) so severe as to require clinical intervention

- pushing down; "depression of the space bar on the typewriter"

Okay, so #4 isn't a "classic" definition of this kind of depression, but I think it works here. There are times when I feel like I have the weight of the world on my shoulders and that's enough to depress anyone! Some days, everything feels like it weighs 20 pounds more. My arms, my eyes, the milk, my feet, and the air... it is much harder to push through with the extra weight. It would be easier to just stay in bed. Overwhelming exhaustion occurs, but sometimes with the inability to sleep. Outrageous thoughts swirl in my head. Everything feels like it's my fault. We are out of toothpaste, my fault. It rained, that's my fault too. My outlook is undeniably pessimistic. Nothing will go right again. Ever. Typing this stuff out...I can see the absurdity of it, but it's what is in my head. How do I help someone who has never had thoughts like these to understand?

My name is Misty and I am clinically and chronically depressed. I am not sure that I will ever be off my SSRIs. But, I am ok with that...most of the time.

There is so much to my story that contributes to my depression. I don't talk about most of this with just anyone, but at my husband's urging, I am going to share.

Depression seems to run in my family. My mom had nine siblings, while two died before I was born, three of her brothers committed suicide. Three of my grandparents were alcoholics as well.

I was not raised in a Christian home, but I had a good home life. I had great parents and never wanted for anything, even though my father wasn't sure how to be a hands-on dad. My depression started when I was a teenager. I think most teenagers go through a rough time, but mine seemed to be especially rough. My 9th grade year in high school was fraught with feelings of inadequacy and I really questioned what my life was all about. It was around this time that I attended a Teen Institute camp. (TI is a teen prevention program... drugs, alcohol, abuse, etc.) I enjoyed several classes, team building exercises and motivational speakers, but I will never forget one in particular. During it, we talked about bad influences and such, but it was when talk came around to strange men doing things to young girls that flood gates opened and suppressed memories came rushing back...I had been sexually molested by my grandfather when I was around 4 or 5. There was a dance that evening at the camp, but I spent the time outside with my counselor trying to come to grips with these emotions that were swirling about in my head. It felt like my life had just changed to be something that I didn't recognize anymore.

Over the next several years, I continued to struggle with these feelings of depression and I started having a lot of anxiety and panic attacks. It got so bad that it was affecting my daily life. I dropped out of college and went through several jobs. It was during all this that I sought treatment. We started with Prozac. I was 18 at the time and there was a huge stigma surrounding it, so we tried several different kinds of medication before I found one I was ok with. I met my fabulous husband, Rich, during all this and I'm thankful to him and to God that he chose to stick by me.

I found that I was really struggling with the memories, so I decided to try some counseling. At this point I also started going to church and I credit this for my sanity. The counseling helped me face my memories so I could put them behind me, but Christ gave me peace. I was able to come off the medication for a while. For once, I felt that I had things figured out and was doing ok. I was even able to forgive my grandfather and had a chance to tell him so before he died.

After a while, I noticed a pattern. I was able to come off my medication during the summer, but needed to start it again around October till about March or April. Rich says that I am solar powered! But I now know that it's Seasonal Affective Disorder or SAD.

Then a whirlwind came along. My husband and I got married. We moved 7 hours away from my family. I had our first child and he died 5 days later. I was put on medication pretty quickly this time. Only by God's grace did we survive this time in our lives. I went on to have another baby, Nicholas, about 18 months later and thought that my life was complete. But he was born in the winter months and I was struck with postpartum depression. I would find myself sobbing in the shower and not remember why. I should have been loving on this amazing creature, but I would leave him lying in the swing while I couldn't get myself off the couch. I was so completely engrossed in trying to get myself together and care for this tiny being that I neglected my husband. My marriage took a blow while I suffered. But I was soon able to get things together and started a job at a Christian daycare. Things looked up again.

Since then, we struggled with secondary infertility before being blessed with our son, Wesley. Then Wesley was diagnosed with autism at the age of two. All I could see was how things were never going to be good again. This beautiful little boy was never going to be able to do the things that I had envisioned and hoped for. Our lives were going to be forever altered and be much harder. What had I ever done to deserve this? I submerged myself in all things autism; it's all I thought about. Again, my family was shoved aside while I tried to make sense of this. I was in a spiral that nothing good could come from.

I slowly, and with the help of my husband and other parents of autistic children, realized that things didn't really change. Wesley was still the same silly little boy that he was before the diagnosis. There was certainly a grieving period for the plans that I unwittingly had for him, but he has taught me to take things in stride. He has been an amazing inspiration for me. He works so hard to learn what should come naturally, and he still has the best sense of humor and makes me laugh daily. I still don't know what the future holds for him, but I know that he's not going to let anything stop him!

I have been on and off medication since 1994, but more on than off, and it's usually not a good idea when I go off it. I am still trying to accept the fact that, just like a diabetic, I have a chronic condition that needs to be treated with medication. It's a daily struggle to push myself. I am learning to seek things that make me step out and pretend sometimes. This pretending will usually lead to learning the behavior and eventually enjoy what I am doing. I signed up to act in my church's children program; I am now a Pampered Chef consultant; I became the registration person for my local MOPS. These are all things that I would never have done, but with my husband's support and God's love, I am able to push back against depression and hold that weight off my shoulders for a little longer.

14

Little Miss Sunshine

by Katie Alicea

I never know when it's going to happen. Sometimes it will hit me when I am in the middle of laughing at a joke. All-of-a-sudden, I'll feel a million miles away even though I am, physically, still in the same location. I feel totally alone even though people surround me. I look at the people I know and I feel like I don't know them anymore. The feeling of panic starts like a wave. It grows in momentum until it finally comes crashing down on me. I break out into a cold sweat. My fight or flight response has been activated for no real reason. I want to run, but I don't want to freak everyone out or look like a crazy person. It takes every drop of energy I have to not run. The world seems to close in on me; wrap itself around me, squeezing so hard I can barely breathe. I wish I could just unzip my skin and run out of the body that has me trapped inside. The inability to calm myself down or talk myself out of this makes me feel like I am on a runaway train. My stomach starts cramping and I get hot. More sweating.

Sometimes I don't know why I start feeling this way and other times I can almost predict that a certain situation will bring it on. Whether or not it is a self-fulfilling prophecy; I'm not sure. No matter the cause, I don't seem to be able to control it. I have managed to learn how to sit or stand there and try to look "normal." As if the panic attacks aren't bad enough, there is also the accompanying depression. Anxiety's BFF. The only way I can describe it is to say that it feels like I am living in a slow moving dark cloud or haze. When people talk about hating to get out of bed to go to work, or talk about feeling too tired to clean their house, I wonder if it is the same intense feeling of exhaustion that I feel when I say those things. I don't hate going to work or cleaning my house, but doing both of those things, sometimes, is so difficult for me to do that I simply can't force myself. I am not one of those people that cry a lot when they are depressed, in fact, I am quite the opposite. I tend to feel numb and apathetic. I can't cry or even feel anything. I just float. This...is my secret.

I've been struggling with anxiety and depression since I was around 9 or 10 years old. In a small town in the early 90's there wasn't much talk of kids with anxiety and depression. There wasn't much talk of anxiety and depression in general. I know now that I wasn't the only one that struggled with these issues as a kid. I was sent to all kinds of doctors and specialists, but no one could make sense of my strange symptoms. I would get hot flashes and break out into a sweat. My chest would start to feel tight and I would feel flashes of panic. My stomach would start cramping and I would have to run to the bathroom over and over again.

I hated going to school because I was so embarrassed by the fact that I felt out of control. I did everything I could to cover up my issue. I didn't go to sleepovers. I didn't have friends over. I even begged my brother not to have friends over. During Christmas or birthdays I would only want my family around and even then I would sometimes stay in my room in my PJs. I couldn't help it that my family knew, but I did all that I could to hide my problem from everyone else.

My physical symptoms were so painful and real that it was hard for my parents to accept that it could all be psychosomatic and a direct result of an anxiety disorder. My parents took me to doctors until someone gave me a diagnosis that made sense to them. How do you look your screaming, crying, and miserable child in the eyes and tell her that her pain is all in her head? Finally, I was diagnosed with possible irritable bowel syndrome and food and environmental allergies, but that didn't make it go away. In fact, it made it worse.

I thought having a name to what plagued me would make it better, but when the medication (Paregoric) the doctors prescribed me still didn't make it all go away I felt like I must be crazy; or worse, broken. Why was I still having the feeling of panic when I had to leave my house? Why did I get hot flashes so bad that I would have to change my clothes from all the sweat? The more my symptoms continued to happen, the harder I worked to hide them. I eventually became an expert at hiding how I felt.

When I left home and went to college I finally went to see a therapist. I was officially diagnosed with major depressive disorder and generalized anxiety disorder when I was 19. I remember my therapist saying that she couldn't believe I had struggled that long without treatment. It was nice to finally have a name for the monster that controlled me, but at the same time it was another secret I had to keep. Therapy never really worked, mainly because I refused to be honest with my therapist. The drugs didn't help either. Even if they helped with the anxiety they made me feel out of it; and I certainly didn't need to feel any more like I was in a cloud. For years I was off and on different medication until I finally gave up on them altogether about 4 years ago. I haven't been to therapy or taken meds for over 4 years.

Not many people know any of this about me. My goal over the last twenty years has been to cover it all up as much as possible. I don't talk about it. I don't blog about it, at least not explicitly. I have become an expert at hiding my secret, even from my own family and friends. I allow very few people to get close enough to me to find this out. It's easier to keep people away than it is to figure out how to hide this fact from people over and over again. Over these last twenty years I have developed my own ways of finding a comfortable way to deal with my anxiety and depression. Being out of control of your feelings and your body is embarrassing, depressing, and exhausting. For years after becoming a Christian I felt guilty or broken because I still struggled with these feelings. I felt that if I could just "pray right" or be "right with God" then all of my issues would go away. The deep emptiness and hopelessness that plagued my youth and young adulthood was mostly gone, but the anxiety and depression still remained...and remains to this day. Literally...today. I am anxious about writing this, because now you know my secret.

The light you see when you meet me or see me isn't fake. That's real. My positivity, joy, and peace isn't fake. It's all real. Most of the time the smile isn't fake. But the joy and peace that come with knowing Jesus doesn't always mean that you will be "happy" or "calm" or not have struggles. Maybe the anxiety and depression remain with me, like a thorn in my side, so that not only will I remain humble, but that I will also be able to always empathize with people that suffer or struggle. I pray to be completely released from it and believe that one day I will. Maybe today. Maybe the secret of it all allowed the depression and anxiety to keep its claws in me. Maybe telling you my secret will take all of its power away and all that remains is the memories and experiences of a battle fought and won. I pray that to be the case. If it's not, then all I have to say is, "In my weakness, He is strong. And He is the purpose for my life."

If you are struggling with anxiety and depression, please know that you are not alone. Feeling like no one can understand or help is one of the most damaging parts of these disorders; and it simply isn't true. You are not alone in your fight. And neither am I. Let today be the day that you stop trying to fight this battle alone. There is hope. There is relief.

15

My Awakening

By Brooke Higinbotham

The wave knocks me down with a force to be reckoned

It comes at me out of nowhere

It thrusts me down to the abrasive floor

It pummels me over and over

I have lost my sense of direction

My eyes are full of needles from trying to find my way

I grasp with blurred vision, for anything to pull myself up

I am thrust down again

I gasp for air, but air does not come-only darkness-then silence

THIS IS DEPRESSION

It is snowing outside; I am staring out of my kitchen window with tears streaming down my face asking myself, how in the world did

I get to this place? I now understand that empty, dead feeling of not wanting to live anymore. I understand for the first time the burning sensation in my gut that just doesn't want to deal with the pain anymore. For years I had been thrusting my true feelings down into some deep dark chasm hoping they would just go away as if to disappear in a black hole never to be dealt with again.

I guess I had always felt my innermost being to be in some type of storm, but I just assumed everyone else felt the same. As an adult who was married with two children, I would tell myself that most people felt the way I did; that it was just a part of this season of raising young children. My insides were churning over the confusion, pain, embarrassment, loneliness, anger and bitterness that accompanied an adult with painful childhood memories. I was a volcano that was on the verge of erupting. I was always on the defense and ready to explode at any given moment.

You see, things started to "kick in" after I had my first son. All of the sudden, I felt the overwhelming urge to protect him from people. This wasn't the normal parental instinct surfacing due to becoming a new parent. I now realized I had to protect him from "the predators". The puzzle pictures in my mind that had started to flash in and out of my life were coming together to create a grim landscape. I had been sexually abused as a child and did not want to admit it or deal with the reality. For about a year and a half I continued to ignore the truth. The joy of another son entered my life along with an increasing "urge to protect". Once again, I refused to deal with the sexual abuse. I attempted to put it in a jar, high on a shelf, so as not to knock it over for fear of what would spill out.

During this time in my life, my husband and I were fairly new Christians. We had thought we were Christians before, but we both had come to the realization (although we didn't discuss it with each other right away) we had not accepted Christ as our savior, our one true God. We had not entered into a relationship with Christ. We had gone to church all of our lives and believed as children, but not with a full understanding as we had recently discovered. This God was the same God that helped us survive the aftermath of previous affairs on both of our parts. He was the same God that loved me unconditionally, regardless of my faults and failures. So, why did I have this gaping open wound that was starting to bleed?

I just couldn't understand the darkness that engulfed me. I would constantly ask myself, "What is wrong with you? You have two beautiful, healthy boys; a great husband; great family, friends and church family." I would blame my pendulum of moods on stress and everyone else around me. As I continued to run our rental business and home school our boys, my world and the kaleidoscope in my mind suffocated me. My mind became more and more jumbled. I was very forgetful (I still am today). If I had taken stock in sticky notes, I'd be a millionaire by now. Disturbing memories haunted me constantly, but especially during sex with my husband. Triggers of the abuse would happen at any given moment. It could be a word, a TV show, a product, smells or a simple brush of the hand from my husband. I was spiraling downward without safety gear. I started to retreat emotionally and physically. I could experience happiness at the surface level, but joy did not enter into my world. The conveyor belt of life kept me moving forward while I watched myself slowly fade away.

During this ten- year period, my life was a paradox. I continued to serve diligently at our church growing in areas of faith and all the while Satan was puncturing my flesh with his fish hooks every chance he could get. I felt I couldn't perform any task at 100% and questioned my abilities as a wife, mother, Christian and as a person in general. My self-esteem hit an all-time low when my husband made it known he was still struggling with a pornography addiction that I thought had long passed and was seeking help through God and accountability partners. Now, all the things I believed had just been confirmed and stabbed me in the heart once again. This time I didn't know if I could get back up again. I believed no one truly loved me; I was never enough, men only wanted to "get off" and I could not trust anyone- not even God.

My anger pressed in and consumed me. I couldn't fathom in the first place how a "loving God" could allow such horrible things to happen to children he supposedly loved. I knew in my heart and mind the lengths I went through to protect my boys from sexual predators. So, if he loved me, then why was I abused? Where the hell was he? Why didn't he stop it from happening? I screamed and cursed at God often asking why was marriage so difficult? Why did he make men and women so different? Why were men so visually oriented? Why was their sex drive typically higher than women's sex drive? Why did we think and communicate so differently? Why was it so hard to have sex with my husband? Why didn't my husband love and respect me? Was our marriage for the past 15 or 16 years just a total lie? All of these thoughts burned in me day and night. I retreated even more emotionally and physically from just about everyone I knew. All I wanted to do was go in my room, pull the curtains and go to sleep. I figured if I was asleep, then I wouldn't have to face reality. I was basically just going through the emotions anyway with fake smiles because that's what we're supposed to do, right? How could a Christian admit they were struggling with their faith and questioning everything about God, especially while serving on a worship team? Didn't everyone in some type of leadership role have it all together? Yeah, right! At one point and time I took a break from serving on the worship team due to my husband and I building a home. (Crazy the things we do when we are just going through the motions.) The last song I sang before my yearlong break was entitled, "How He Loves." I will never forget the moment I finished the song and practically ran off the stage in tears asking God if he truly loved me. It was at that moment I felt the least loved at all in my life.

So, this is how I ended up at my kitchen window watching the white crystals caress my lawn as my vision in the black tunnel got smaller and smaller. I looked at the intricate details of the jumbo flakes and thought, "If God created this beautiful snow with such detail, than surely a human life was worth living." My mind drifted back to a conversation I had with a girlfriend one summer at the beach. I had been discussing with her my struggles and she shared with me how a Christian marriage counselor had tremendously helped her and her husband not only together, but individually as well. With that memory awakened in my thoughts I decided at that moment I could no longer travel this road on my own. My mind and body were suffering with pain that I couldn't tolerate anymore. It was time to reach out for help.

I started with the counselor hired by my church. We had a couple sessions then he referred me to a psychologist he knew that happened to be a Christian. I specifically wanted a Christian counselor because I knew I was having a spiritual crisis as well as emotional crisis. I don't doubt at all that some secular counselors are great, but I wanted to be able to keep God in the discussions. She and I had a few sessions of tests and talking.

After about a couple months she felt I was dealing with a level of depression, but primarily was struggling with anger, intimacy and trust issues. She referred me to Barnabas Ministry. This ministry for me was truly a Godsend. I am still involved with this ministry today on a regular basis. It is in a very casual setting, so you are already at ease when you walk in the door. I am welcomed with open arms. I am able to express my thoughts about God whether positive or negative without any judgment placed upon me. I am cradled by not only their loving arms, but with their prayers and honesty during discussions. They have a plethora of information to study via books, videos, CDs and DVDs. I am given biblical truths along with encouragement to seek biblical truths. I am assisted in sorting out the truth from Satan's lies and recognizing that believing Satan's lies about self worth are destructive physically, emotionally and spiritually. Over the past couple years through Barnabas Ministry and from the prayers of friends and family, I have begun to come out of my darkness. Right now I have not accomplished who or all I want to be, but I am thankful I am not where I used to be.

16

The Panic Room

By Joanna Ross

It was about 2 AM when I woke up, gasping for air. My chest felt as if it was being crushed. My body was paralyzed. The beating of my heart was deafening and seemed to race out of control. Was I having a heart attack? An asthma attack? A stroke? A seizure? I was terrified to close my eyes. I blinked. My eyes darted toward my bedroom door, but I couldn't even open my mouth to call for help. I felt like I was choking. The heaviness on my chest surrounded me like a lead straightjacket. There seemed to be a sinkhole in my bed, and I was being sucked into it. Only I couldn't fight it. I could only feel myself slowly sinking into it. I was sure I was about to die.

Suddenly, I was no longer being pulled down, but lifted up. I was experiencing depersonalization, which is when you feel completely detached from your body. I looked down and watched myself as if I were in a dream. It was almost two hours until my body began to calm and I was able to move and speak. It was petrifying to feel a complete loss of control over my own body as I lay, trapped in my own little panic room.

That was my first panic attack. I was fourteen years old at that time. It was the worst I ever experienced, but not the last. I'd all ready had problems with depression for a year or two before the anxiety episodes began. I'd been really happy and enjoying school at that age. Chronic stomachaches and migraines caused me to miss quite a bit of school. My headaches and stomachaches became notorious in the family. I missed enough school that I was given a "While You Were Out" notepad as a joke from the student council I served on. I constantly worried that I was on the verge of "losing it." I felt that surely someone would look right through me and see the fakeness I radiated and see how unhappy I was beneath. There didn't seem to be some obvious cause to the sadness either. I was doing well in school, no problems at home, and I mostly looked forward to school each day. Yet, everyday, I was exhausted when I woke up and spent much of the time lying in bed or writing in my journal at home. I was too tired just getting through each day to deal with trying to explain how badly I felt to my family. I quit telling family what was going on. It seemed easier just to keep it to myself than to burden my family with my plethora of ailments. The anxiety and depression were a secret shame I kept to myself, gradually accepting they were just part of who I was. The exhaustion was the thing that really stands out to me about this time in my life. Exhaustion and feeling overwhelmed. This is how I felt all the time.

Though anxiety and depression came and went many times since then, in 2010, I was diagnosed with an adrenal disorder that has been a major cause of my anxiety and depression for seventeen years. The adrenal issue was cured in less than two months of treatment. The exhaustion has given way to feeling refreshed and looking forward to waking up in the morning. I haven't had as much of a problem with anxiety as I used to, but when I feel the panic setting in, I can recognize it for what it is. Today the anxiety and depression aren't entirely gone but I feel more like the old me again.

If you are having problems with anxiety and depression, **please don't make the same mistake I did**. Don't assume that people are too busy to care. Don't assume that there is nothing that you can do. Don't waste years of your life thinking this is as good as it gets. Don't buy into the notion that you are weak or crazy or a disgrace simply because you have a chemical imbalance. There are many different causes for depression. My issues were made worse by the fact that I had a medically -induced problem that was making my anxiety and depression worse. Don't give into the exhaustion and just accept anxiety or depression will dictate your life.

Most people don't understand that anxiety and depression can't just be "snapped" out of. You lose control of your body. Just as you can't physically stop a heart attack by wishing it gone, you can't just hope your depression away. You wouldn't hesitate to be rushed to the hospital if you were having a heart attack. So if your life has been hijacked by anxiety or depression, there are people and treatments available to help you take back control- whether it is Zoloft, therapy, breathing techniques or herbal supplements.

Don't live your life in a panic room.

17

In The Moment

By Mary Balfoort

I'm finally sitting down to write this on the eve of my 49th birthday. I've missed one deadline for submission so far and have been having conversations with myself (in my head) about why I haven't sat down and written about my depression. I actually started to write about it, got as far as two paragraphs and left it sit. I didn't like how I started it; it felt too stilted, so I kept trying to think of a way to begin my story in a different way.

And then I began to think about a deeper reason as to why putting my story about depression into the written word was intimidating for me. It meant that I was going public in a huge way about depression, MY depression and it meant that I really need to face this, more so than I think I ever have in all the time I have been suffering/dealing/hating/coping/living with depression.

Looking back, I'd say I probably was depressed on and off since I was a kid. Back in the late 1960's – the 1970's, depression wasn't talked about, especially if you were a kid trying to figure out what the hell was wrong with you, why you didn't feel happy all the time, why it was hard to get motivated. Add in parents who fought (violently at times) with their marriage ending in divorce, being the oldest of two children in a family with a history (on both sides of the family) of depression, alcohol abuse in a time when none of this was talked about, it's a recipe for depression.

Fast forward to college, sophomore year – the friends I had the year before had been seniors and had graduated. I suddenly felt very alone. I slept a lot. I would get to the cafeteria last and leave first. Stomach issues ensued. A friend a couple of years older than me finally convinced me to seek therapy. It wasn't that easy of course, I felt I didn't need therapy, I was the strong one, I was a problem solver, I could handle this, and bless her, she countered all of those answers and persevered until I realized she was right and I needed help.

I was a wreck when I asked a Psychology professor who was also a therapist for help. I walked around campus after setting up the appointment feeling like everyone knew I was crazy, which is how I felt then.

I've been in therapy on and off since then. It's been helpful and some of the therapists have been good and some better. But really, when I really look at my past I have to face up to the fact that I have been living with depression for over 30 years and it's not going anywhere fast. It's become my sidekick, sometimes a step behind, but always, always there, shadowing me. I have had some times in the past when I did ok without therapy or drugs, but I'm afraid that those days are gone for me. As I have gotten older I must look in the mirror and realize that I must learn to live with it and that is a hard fact that's difficult at times to face. Now I need to work with my doctor and find the right mixture of prescription drugs to help me get through the days. It's not only depression, but I've dealt with anxiety attacks in the last 10 years, not knowing what they were at first, but when the anxiety attacks got really bad, it was horrid for me and for my wife. I felt out of control, lost and like I was having mini nervous breakdowns, mostly at the job I had at the time. The job was also stressful at the time and my poor wife received so many phone calls from me in tears, wanting to quit, feeling trapped because of us needing me to work.

Depression/anxiety is rough, and I can't imagine what my wife has had to go through dealing with me and my sidekick. I'm grateful every day that I have her support and for the many times she has listened and just lets me be to work through it, letting me know she is that light at the end of my very long dark tunnel.

It's not a bed of roses for people like me who will have to live with depression/anxiety for the rest of our lives. I've tried not being on the prescription drugs in the past and I've always, always had to come back to them. I'm on a decent combo right now and am functioning pretty well on them. Occasionally stress or some other stimuli will overwhelm me, but the episodes don't last as long as they use to. Please don't misunderstand, those episodes are still rough to get through, I don't like the person I am when going through them, I become very intense and often short tempered and verbalizing what's going on becomes extremely difficult.

As I'm writing this, I am constantly thinking that writing about this is like coming out of the closet when a person is gay. Only for me, being a late-in-life lesbian was easier to deal with than putting my depression down on paper. There seems to me to be a huge stigma about depression – how will people view me once they know? Will it affect my job (which I love right now)? I don't tell a lot of people about it (that's a moot point now!) because a lot of people don't know how to react to someone who is depressed and lives with depression on a daily basis. I've heard all the responses of 'pick yourself up' and 'pull yourself up by the bootstraps' and 'it will get better' and 'tomorrow's another day' ad nausea.

The one thing about being someone who has lived with depression this long is that I have learned how much of an extrovert I can be and when to draw back in and be a homebody. It's an ebb and flow process and I have to watch myself because some days I would rather cocoon at home than go out and that sometimes can lead to a worse depression.

So how am I going to deal with the fact that there will be people from everywhere reading my story in this book? I'm going to face it, like so many other hurdles in my life, the best I can at this time and place in my life. I will probably still be cautious with people I know around me, but I'm going try to look at it like I did when I faced breast cancer nine years ago, that if my story can help just one person, then it was worth making myself vulnerable and putting myself out there. We never know whom we may touch in our journey called life, and I've been blessed to know that I have in fact touched people in my past.

With that, my name is Mary Balfoort and I live with depression and anxiety and I'm going to live with it day to day and the best that I can in that moment.

18

Rage Against The Baby

By Robin Farr

I've never struggled with depression.

Except... Oh wait. There was that time in the last semester of my first year of university when I spent a lot of time in bed. A LOT. I stayed there and didn't want to get up, though I didn't think much of it at the time.

Then when I was in my 20s, I got sick of feeling sad and hopeless all the time and started logging things. What I ate, exercise, weather – you name it, I put it into a carefully crafted spreadsheet, and it was all mapped against my mood. Eventually the sum of the things that made me feel better – getting enough exercise, sunlight, eating well – led me to feel better overall.

Those times, I wasn't diagnosed with depression. I never even had a conversation with a doctor about it. I always hated that label. Oddly, though, I remember being asked to fill out a self-identification form for a previous job. "Are you a visible minority?" No. "Are you Aboriginal?" No. "Do you have a disability?" A very small voice in my head piped up. "Does depression count?" I knew it was there, though I was never willing to admit it. (I checked no.)

Then I had a baby and it was way harder than I expected it to be. I didn't know I was experiencing postpartum depression because I didn't feel sad. I was just angry all the time, without knowing anger is a symptom of depression. I was so resistant to the label I didn't allow myself to consider it anyway.

Case in point: In February 2009 my son was eight months old and I wasn't doing very well. He didn't sleep well ("Screamfest 2009" I think we dubbed it) and I was so tired I seemed to have totally lost my ability to cope. I decide to see a counselor, so I called the Employee & Family Assistance Program provided through my work. I told them I was a new mom struggling with some issues and wanted to talk to someone about it. They referred me to a counselor, who called to find out more about what I was looking for. I told her my story – fussy baby, not sleeping, feeling overwhelmed, etc. etc.

"Sounds like you're suffering from postpartum depression," she said.

"No," I said. Emphatically. "It's not that. I'm really not interested in calling it that. I just need to SLEEP."

I'm sure her first thought was something along the lines of, "Oh, this one's going to be fun" but she gamely set up an appointment to see me.

I went for my first session and talked about my issues. I cried. A LOT.

"I really think you're dealing with PPD," she said again. "You probably need to see your doctor."

I wasn't interested. Didn't listen.

All credit to this counselor – she had me figured out: professionally successful and used to feeling competent and in control. A tendency to be hard on myself. Dealing with unrealistic expectations. And dealing with PPD and totally unwilling to admit it or talk to someone about whether medication might help.

I spent every session talking to her and crying my eyes out. After each hour I had a handful of little wet, balled up Kleenexes, a blotchy face and the knowledge that I was going home to a kid who, if he was asleep at all, was going to wake up throughout the night and scream his adorable little face off.

I continued to see her for about six weeks. It helped a little, I suppose, but was more exhausting than anything else and I didn't need any help being tired. The last time I saw her I told her I'd call her to schedule my next appointment. I never did, of course. She did call me – a couple of times. I know she was concerned and genuinely trying to help. But I told her I was okay and waited for the problem to go away.

Fast forward to December 2010. In the intervening two years, I'd seen five doctors and three counselors. After some reading, I'd come to terms with the PPD label and had asked for a referral to someone a friend told me about – a psychiatrist who specializes in postpartum disorders – but I didn't meet the criteria to see her (having a child under one year or being pregnant). I'd looked into a counselor, recommended by this same friend, who runs a PPD program, but I didn't meet the criteria for a referral to her either. So I'd given up, decided to stay on the meds I'd been prescribed, and crossed my fingers.

One Monday early in December 2010, my son woke at 4:30 a.m. and refused to go back to sleep. We'd had a rough patch of sleep in the previous few weeks and the early wake-up put me over the edge. I had one of those mornings where I could barely get myself out the door to work, then finally got there and realized I'd left my travel mug of badly needed tea in my car. I went into my office, shut the door, buried my face in my hands and cried.

After that day – where the lack of sleep tipped me over into a full-on scary PPD place again, where forgotten tea prompted a breakdown – I decided to make the call I'd been putting off. I called the counselor who specializes in PPD and agreed to fork over the money to see her as a private client.

At my first appointment, I told her why I was there and still couldn't do it without bawling. I need someone who specializes in this to tell me if I'm nuts or not. Is this normal? Can it be dealt with?

She listened quietly, patiently. When I was done she paused, as if waiting for more, and then said she'd tell me what she thinks.

"I think you're dealing with postpartum depression," she said.

I cried with relief. Finally, someone was telling me what was wrong with me.

And that time I listened.

After that I started to acknowledge my past episodes of depression in conversations with doctors and counselors, but it wasn't until I talked about it with a psychiatrist in the spring of 2011 that I really began to realize that I've been dealing with depression for a lot of my adult life.

Some days I feel great and some days I feel like I'm getting sucked back into the hole. I'm waiting to be "recovered" from PPD, but I don't know if it works that way if I'm prone to depression anyway. Maybe this is my new reality, and I'm just going to have to deal with it.

Ironically, one of the biggest things that's helped me is that I've named this depression now. I've allowed it to attach itself to me. No, better – I've attached it to myself, and I've accepted it as part of who I am.

19

Peace Be With You

By Jake Kampe

The stigma of depression in our culture makes it somewhat of a taboo to discuss. Christians who deal with depression are often ostracized, ignored or accused of having weak faith. I've even heard some imply that I cannot truly be a follower of Christ, let alone a pastor since I deal with depression. *"You know, Jake, depression is a curse from God,"* has always been my favorite explanation. A very interesting concept, considering the depth of depression that King David suffered, and yet what was he called? Oh yeah, *"a man after God's own heart" (1 Samuel 13:14 NIV)*. I confess that I've felt abandoned by God, felt that I had pissed Him off, even felt that He was punishing me for one of my many screw-ups in life. But I never felt that He had somehow divinely cursed me with the burden of depression.

To say that I have lived with depression is an understatement. To say that I've seen glimpses of Hell is much more accurate. To say that fear is a companion emotion of depression is not quite the right description. Terror that has brought me to the brink of contemplating suicide is much more illustrative. When I meditate on the landscape that has been my journey through this world, depression has been right there with me, every step of the way. You might say that it's been an unwelcome traveling companion. As far back as I can remember depression has made itself comfortable with almost every aspect of my life. During major life decisions, crossroads or milestones that have occurred in my life, depression has been there, reminding me that I have to engage in a consultation before proceeding.

When I was very young, I vividly remember periods of unusual depression. I may not have realized the full magnitude of what was taking place in my psyche, but the seeds were being planted, the soil was being cultivated, and roots were beginning to form. The dark cloud of despair was beginning to form itself around my soul and would eventually contribute to molding me into the person I am today. Depression was introducing itself and settling into a comfortable place that would eventually develop into a long stay.

I live with depression; I also live with peace. The two go hand in hand, and although they do not live side by side in complete unity, they've learned to accept one another. Peace usually dominates the relationship these days, but occasionally depression takes the upper hand. Depression knows peace's weaknesses and although peace is much stronger, wiser and rational, occasionally depression outsmarts peace and takes temporary control of the household. For a brief period of time, depression wreaks havoc and can quickly destroy a lot of what peace has built. The relationship between the two has not always been this way. Not so long ago, depression was the dominant force in the relationship. In fact, there were long periods of time when peace was forced to leave. Remaining in isolation and forced seclusion, I wondered if peace would ever return.

Being part of a church always provided me with some much needed normality. I was raised in the Roman Catholic Church. The traditions and rituals brought comfort and stability into a life that seemed to be becoming increasingly unstable. Most people were loving and caring, especially during the traditional greeting of, *"Peace be with you."* I'm sure that in many instances it's extended with a certain amount of ritual and habit, but to me it was warm and comforting, especially from those older than me. *"Peace be with you, Jake"* they would say. "Yes!", I thought to myself. "Peace *be* with *me*. Please, God".

As the years passed, I became increasingly isolated and began to reject most attempts of friendship and expressions of love. Throughout junior high and high school, manifestations of depression resulted in bouts of anger and frustration. In my attempts to control the debilitating and helpless effects of depression, anger became my weapon of choice. Anger was more controllable. Anger was *my* decision to unleash and more controllable. It was mine, and in many ways it kept me warm from the chills of depression. One evening in particular, my best friend at the time was the recipient of my self-defense mechanism. Trying in vain to encourage me, he continued to plead with me to talk about what I was going through. Exhausted with despair and his constant attempts to miraculously heal my emotional state, I exploded. The throwing of a fist and desk chair quickly led him to realize that his effort were useless and also realize that my life was more out of control than he imagined. I fended off depression for yet another day, sharpened my weapon for future battles and isolated myself further. Not exactly the method Dr. Phil would recommend.

As I grew older, and depression became deeper, I began to see that it often distorts reality. Not only does it seem to affect the emotions of one's internal make up, it also emotionally manipulates the external. There is no physical manifestation of the changes that depression initiates. No one else can see what the mind's eye witnesses. But nonetheless, for the person dealing with the onslaught of severe depression, things just don't seem the same. Reality becomes twisted, contorted and dreamlike. Nightmarish, unreal and even sometimes hallucinogenic was my reality.

Toward the end of college, I felt as though my life was in full-blown crisis. Regular cocktails of anti-depressants, downers and alcohol only numbed the pain that was hiding just below the surface. The temporary alleviation of suffering created a false reality that only isolated me further. "Nothing seems real to me anymore" I remember telling my psychologist at the time. He immediately said with certainty, "Then Jake, you need to be in a place where things can feel real again." What was he saying? Did I need to be in a hospital? Institutionalized? Was I that bad off? I don't remember much of those days, but I remember that moment very well. It was a sobering realization that my life had spiraled out of control. One question remained: Where was God in the midst of this downward journey into an unknown abyss?

Even attending church, spending time in prayer or reading scripture became an uncomfortable experience. I suppose that even my image of God was distorted, but ironically my faith was growing deeper. My convictions to know Him more fully and serve Him were growing as well. But like a car stuck in the mud, the more I spun the wheels of effort and faith, the deeper I seemed to sink. My prayers became mundane, spiritless and forced. I would frequently find it hard to focus on God and my anger and frustration soon became directed more toward Him. I began to envision God mockingly holding the key to my healing. Dangling it just beyond my reach, He would smile as I reached out.

If God loved me so much, why was He allowing me to suffer such a hellish existence?   If He was real, why was He so apparently unwilling to lift me out of this despair?   What possible good could my depression be accomplishing for Him and His Kingdom? Hebrews 13:5 & 6 says *"Never will I leave you; never will I forsake you"* "Really, God?   Then where are you?   Are you hiding from me?   Playing games?"   *"I came that they may have life, and have it abundantly"* *(John 10:10 NASB).*   "Then what is this miserable pit in which I'm living?"   *"Weeping may last through the night, but joy comes with the morning"?*   *(Psalm 30:5 NLT).*   "Interesting, because the only morning visitors I ever had were fear and panic, God.   Where is this joy you promised I am supposed to have?"   *"Peace I leave with you; my peace I give you?"* *(John 14:27, NIV).*   "Bullshit!"

But life continued on and I eventually met my wife who got to experience my ordeals first hand.   In reality, I know that there were times when she contemplated leaving me to escape the nightmare that we now both shared.   But by God's grace, she remained by my side, as faithful and understanding as she could be.   Ironically, in the long run depression strengthened our relationship, and we grew closer.   My two sons came into the world and we began to build the family and life we had longed for.   Despite the added stress and responsibility, becoming a father actually helped me deal with depression.   Maybe it was because the focus shifted more from me and toward others that I loved.   Maybe it was because I was learning and growing spiritually.   Maybe it was because God was showing me that my life was actually blessed, rather than cursed.   Either way, my children were a turning point for me.   A much needed light in a long period of darkness.

I awoke early on Easter Sunday of 2000 with a full blown,

unexpected and unprovoked panic attack. In a cold sweat and with heart racing, I got out of bed and went for a walk just before the sun came up. As I walked, I began to pray. As I prayed, my pace increased to a run. As I ran, I began to scream at God in anger. As I screamed, I fell on the grass and broke down. I cried out to God, "Please, God! Stop this! Please! Free me from this hell that I'm in! I can't do it anymore! What do I do? What have I done wrong? Please help me!"

God's response? Clearly and almost audible, I heard Him say, *"Be obedient, Jake."* "What?" I thought to myself. Be *obedient?*" At this point in my life, I had developed a regular prayer life, was involved in church, read my Bible and jumped through every freaking Christian hoop I could think of! How else could I be more *obedient?* "Be obedient to WHAT, God?" I cried out. He softly responded, *"Just be obedient. You're not being obedient."* "I give up, God. You're not going to help me. You've abandoned me. I guess I'm on my own!" I punched the ground and wept as the sun came up. "He is Risen!" I couldn't care less on that Easter Sunday.

I look at this as my moment of healing, but there's nothing magical that happened in me. No immediate change occurred in my soul, but as the days passed I meditated on what God meant. I realized that obedience had nothing to do with my feelings. It had nothing to do with my actions. And it really had nothing to do with me at all. What God revealed to me was that even though depression had taken over my life, it didn't get me off the hook. He still wanted me to live as His child, free from darkness and fear. Depression and fear have no place in Kingdom of God, so I needed to show others just the opposite, even though I didn't feel it. As I began to basically "fake it", something interesting happened. I began to *feel* it. As others perceived me to be healed, I essentially was. As I became obedient, God did as well and peace found me again. That was over ten years ago and although I still struggle with depression, it doesn't control me.

As bizarre as it may seem, I've found a way to thank God for depression. I see that it's helped me become a better husband, father and even a better pastor. I'm now able to not only sympathize with people, but I can also empathize. I feel the pain that others feel and it becomes real to me, so much so that I find myself wanting to avoid it. "God, please don't make me go down this path with this person. The pain is too real. It's too familiar." But each time He reminds me that I'll be OK. *"Go with them. Feel their pain, Jake. This is not your life anymore, but you have to feel it with them now. It's essential to your connection with them."*

So, I feel it. It hurts. My heart begins to race and I feel a cold sweat break out over my body. But I feel it with anyone who needs me to join them and I offer peace to be with them. As I feel their pain, I also feel peace rise inside of me, and as we share this common duality of emotions, the Kingdom of God becomes just a little more real for both of us. Peace be with you.

20

Blue Daisy

By Jody Johnson

I have lived with depression for over 30 years now. For much of that time I had no words to express what I was experiencing, or why I was different from other people. Even after my diagnosis at age 29, I believed that if I learned more skills for navigating my illness I would eventually be free to live a "normal" life; that I would be more acceptable to the outside world. So I took classes in stress management and conflict resolution, learned the politics of the county government I worked for, learned to carefully read the emotions of other people around me. I was kind to my coworkers and advocated for my clients—and I still had depression. I will never forget the day when I suddenly realized that all I had been doing was "window-dressing", trying to change my external behavior, while not changing my internal make up one bit. I was who I was from the inside out, and there was no changing that. It was a devastating realization for me, because it carried with it the belief that I would never be acceptable to the vast majority of people around me, that there was really no hope I could have any kind of satisfying life, or truly be loved as I was.

That day was five years ago, and I've come to the conclusion that I was only partially correct in my interpretation. I do think that I am intrinsically different in "how my brain is wired" than people who don't have depression. I feel things very intensely, and am very sensitive to not only my own moods, but the moods and emotions of others.   My illness is treatable, but chronic; and my baseline mood may always be lower than the baseline mood of others around me. In a field of dandelions, I will never be a dandelion. I like to think of myself as more of a blue daisy: unusual and striking, but still appealing in my own way.

Letting go of trying to be like everyone else has had its own kind of freedom. Now I try and concentrate more on how I can use what I have to the best advantage. In my career as a social worker, my ability to sense even subtle shifts in the emotions of other people has helped me to relate better to my clients. My realization of how it feels to be different from "the norm" gives me perspective when I work with clients who often feel different from the norm themselves in a variety of ways. I am able to meet them "where they're at" and work with them to move forward in their lives, without judging or shaming them. My illness has prepared me in a unique way to listen intently to the pain and experiences of other people, without flinching.   My clients sense that, and it makes our work together more productive and more deeply authentic.

My depression can sometimes take a toll on my personal relationships, however. When I begin to feel the darkness of my depression increasing, I sometimes seek out comfort from friends and family that they are not prepared to give. The internal isolation and sheer emotional weight of my illness can lead me to ask for more time, more attention, more affirmation and affection- sometimes resulting in people backing away from me when I need them the most. It has been a process learning to help myself through these times, learning to gauge when I feel the most vulnerable and finding ways to soothe myself. On very draining workdays, I sometimes take a longer lunch hour and get a manicure, for example, or go to the health club and work myself into a sweat when I am feeling over stimulated or angry. I may retreat to my car for 30 minutes with a good thriller novel to clear my head, or find a quiet place to write. At home, I may seek out one of my cats or my German shepherd to sit with until I am calmer- my animals seem to have a unique ability to give unconditional affection, and unlike many human beings, are unfazed by the intensity of my mood.

One thing I've found particularly helpful is seeking out experiences that give me joy. As someone with depression, my underlying mood is not generally euphoric; but certain experiences evoke a kind of visceral joy in me for a brief time. Finding and claiming those moments in my life has been very healing for me. The feel of the wind on my face as I ride on the back of a dear friend's motorcycle, the energy of taking part in a social justice rally, the rush of finding exactly the right words for a poem or other piece of writing. Passionate, creative moments that bring light into my own personal darkness. I also try to surround myself with small pleasures- flowers on my desk, scented candles or soothing incense at home, an occasional indulgence in really good chocolate fudge or raspberry ice cream. Sometimes it is the details in life that make all the difference, that give me the hope and strength to make it through one more day.

Another source of strength and joy for me is the relationships I have with my closest friends and loved ones. Going out for coffee with a friend and talking for hours, taking a road trip with a coworker, visiting the art show of a friend or family member all give me moments of belonging that interrupt my isolation, and lift my spirits. A shared joke, meaningful look or affectionate hug can warm me for hours, and remind me that I am not truly alone, even if I often feel that I am. My illness has taught me to pay close attention to the emotional cues of others, allowing me to be more sensitive and empathic with the people closest to me. It has also taught me to listen intently to the sound of other people's pain, without retreating or feeling uncomfortable. My friends know that they can talk to me about a variety of very intimate subjects, and I will not judge or reject them. This is the gift of living with depression: the ability to experience intense feelings from others or myself without turning and running, the ability to share intimate moments with another human being, without bursting into flames, or into uncontrollable tears.

Depression has taught me to slow down, and watch. To observe the many ways that people communicate. I used to be very impatient with "small talk", feeling that it was shallow and pointless when I wanted to discuss the deeper problems of the world. I came to realize that every person communicates a little differently, and that if I watched their patterns of relating I could learn something about them; learn the hidden meanings behind their words and actions. One man I know communicates in actions, and uses very few words. He listens to the needs that people express and then tries to do something concrete about those needs- building a shelf, making a meal, fixing a car. The depth of his affection is very real and very present, but it is seldom verbal. His emotional "language" is different than mine, but I have learned to hear it loud and clear, and appreciate it. If I had not lived all these years with depression, I might have missed the meaning of his actions entirely, never heard the subtle tones of his caring for others.

I've come to the conclusion that this illness is a life long journey. It keeps me humble; it is hard to be arrogant for any length of time when this illness frequently reminds me of my fragile humanity. It has made me strong, because I have to keep developing my inner resources to deal with it. It has forced me to face my deepest fears-of being abandoned, being alone, being found unworthy by those I love the most- and to move past them. It has taught me to love deeply without losing myself in the process, and to accept what and who I am without judgment. Living with this illness has given me the ability to listen compassionately and intently to other people, and to comfort them when they are in pain, as only one who has experienced deep pain can.

I've learned to be content with being a blue daisy instead of a dandelion. My life may not be the "norm", but I can make good use of the gifts I have. I can contribute something to my work, my friends, my family that is uniquely mine, and meaningful. I can create, laugh, and love; I can share my experiences with other people, and hopefully lessen some of their emotional burden in the process. As a blue daisy, I still have something to give the world, even if I will never be the dandelion I had hoped to be five years ago. I can let go now of "needing to be normal", and simply be the blue daisy that I was from the beginning, and will continue to be.

21

Redemption Begins at the Scrap Heap

By Kristin Tennant

I'll never forget the first time someone asked if I might be depressed.

I was mourning the loss of so much in my life and was crying inconsolably, almost daily. Yet somehow when Karen, who had come over to rescue me (again), asked, "Do you think you might be depressed?" my first impulse was "No way! Me?" After all, I got out of bed each day and managed to shower, take care of my kids, do my work. I wasn't eating too much, or too little. I wasn't suicidal. Certainly I couldn't be depressed! Wouldn't I know if I was?

That's the way depression is: sly and sneaky. It slips into your life when you're not looking. Maybe you're distracted by big changes that are out of your control, or you're busy applying veneer to your life—the sort that will fool everyone else into thinking your existence is something it isn't. Either way, you're preoccupied, so you don't notice Depression when it enters without knocking and takes up residence in an unused, cluttered corner of your world.

At first, Depression mostly keeps to itself, taking up very little space, almost never in the way. Depression knows how to play the considerate houseguest. But gradually it starts to unpack and spread out, leaving a trail of it's ugliness across your scrubbed existence. Depression is the master of the gradual *everything*. The weightiness, the pressure, is a cloud that gathers so gently you're conditioned to its presence and growth. You hardly notice it, and maybe, if you do, you dismiss it as a minor irritation you can live with.

Maybe distance is the only way to detect depression. You have to back far enough away from it to see the havoc it has wrecked— the mess it is making. My friend Karen had that distance, because although she was right there, observing my life, she wasn't *in* my life. I have that distance too, now that I'm taking refuge on the other side. But I'm getting ahead of myself.

In my case, it's much easier to pinpoint the moment the *word* "depression" entered my life, than it is to put my finger on the moment depression itself arrived. My mom might say now, in retrospect, that it arrived for me with puberty, but that time in my life is too fuzzy for me to have any real perspective on. So when did it slip in?

Each person who struggles with depression eventually learns to identify personal red flags. From my "enlightened" perspective now, helplessness, indecision, and a turning inward define my depression—all emotions that have nothing to do with who I am when I'm at my best. As one who was typically decisive, opinionated and outgoing, I was alarmed when those opposing traits began to take hold, after my first baby was born. At the time I blamed exhaustion and my lack of confidence in my mothering abilities, but now I know it was more.

When I was seven months pregnant with my second baby, and in the process of making plans for my daughter's second birthday party, I fell apart. My marriage was falling apart then, too, and I felt trapped—held hostage not only by my Christian upbringing and the expectations of people who loved me, but also by my dependence on my husband's help and income. Divorce simply wasn't an option, so I was determined to carry on.

I'll never forget that moment when I first felt my determination dissolve under me. I was sitting on the orange love seat in the sunroom of my first, very-own home, with my beautiful toddler daughter playing nearby and this miraculous new life growing inside of me. I called my mom, crying so hard I couldn't begin to tell her what was wrong, not that I really knew. She told me to sit where I was—she was coming to get me. My mom made the hour-and-a-half drive to my house, helped me pack up a few things my daughter and I would need, and then ferried us safely back to my childhood home for a few days. As we drove along the curvy two-lane highway, blankets of January snow spreading out on either side, she told me not to worry about anything, urging me to eat the dark chocolate she had brought because "it was good for me." I was numb, relieved to let go of my concerns and be cared for, yet I didn't know what I was experiencing. I had so many other names for it, so many excuses and distractions. "Depression" still didn't enter my thoughts, even though it had taken up residence in my chemistry.

The post-partum depression that struck after the birth of my second daughter was a different beast—it was about dullness more than sadness. I didn't know it then, of course. I only knew I hadn't felt truly alive in a very long time. I saw the life in my baby, who was a joy—so much easier than her sister had been. Sometimes I looked at her, lying contentedly on a blanket on the floor, watching the action, and her contentment alone made me cry. She was so innocent—so sweet. At certain moments, as I walked through the dull numbness of those tired days, it seemed she was the only thing in my life that was vivid—the only thing for me rather than against me.

My husband and I had started marriage counseling before the baby was born, and we knew we had to somehow continue to fit it into our schedule, even with two little ones, his full-time job and my part-time job. He was every bit as unhappy as I was—frustrated by needs I had that he couldn't meet, worn out by a job he didn't love, and unable to find time to work in his studio, creating his art and feeding his introvert's needs. When he first told me about an open teaching job in a small, Midwestern university town, I flatly refused. "I'm not moving there," I said. "I love our house, I love my job. I have friends here—I'm close to my family and their support."

But a few weeks later, while listening to a sermon at church, I had an epiphany of sorts. What if this job—the possibility of a move—was the key to fixing our marriage and our life? Maybe if my husband was happy, I would be happy—we would *all* be happy! Everything would actually *feel* the way I had been trying to make it look.

It was a year later, in my home in that small university town, when Karen asked if I thought I was depressed. The previous 12 months had contained not just a move, but also more arguments with my husband, more counseling, more misery, helplessness and indecision. There had been many, many more tears, and fewer friendships and support. Sure, my marriage wasn't a mess in its own right, and moving away from home and parenting a toddler and a baby definitely put a strain on your life. But now I understand that depression took everything that was hard—everything that was wrong—and gave it a depth and intensity I couldn't manage. On their own, each of those problems was just two-dimensional—easy enough to sort, stack and file away, like a pile of mail cluttering the dining room table. But depression took the problems— each argument, each frustrating day of parenting, each pang of homesickness—and gave them shape and stature and power over me. It brought all of those problems to life, stacking them up until they towered over me, and I cowered, paralyzed.

What's amazing to me now—almost a decade after I started taking anti-depressants and sensing some relief—is how long I walked down that dark path as if it was normal. I'm not saying I thought it was fun or pretty—not for a second. But I did somehow think it was my lot in life, walking through each day as if weighted down, held back from being the person I was created to be, incapable of doing the things I was meant to do. We have an amazing capacity to convince ourselves that whatever we're experiencing is "normal." It's a survival mechanism, I'm sure—this ability to accept and adapt to what is and incorporate it into our lives—but the mental acrobats we perform to help us carry on can also do us in. Something has to snap us out of the life of dull monotones, giving us the perspective we need to see our lives in bright, vivid detail once again.

For me, even all the crying, all the not-knowing what I wanted, had become "normal." It took a friend uttering the word I had not uttered—depression—to get me to jump the endless tracks I was on, and shift toward the possibility of something different.

Once I had left that place, though, the idea of going back, even for one day, terrified me. I had somehow survived life with depression, week after week, month after month, but the thought of what had been "normal" then became excruciating.

I know exactly how much the idea terrified me; because a year after being on anti-depressants, when it was time to renew my prescription, I thought I was "better" and would stop taking them. At my doctor's instruction, I began weaning myself off my 20mg dose, taking one every other day, and then every few days. By the time I was down to just a couple pills in the bottom of the bottle, I was experiencing moments that might as well have been visits from the ghosts of my past, or glimpses back into a nightmare world I had narrowly escaped. I called my doctor's office and begged the nurse, sobbing and pleading, to renew my prescription immediately.

This decision to go off the drugs is an odd, but I suspect common, one. We so desperately want to believe we can be "healed"—that we simply experienced a brief detour in our lives, a small problem that can be "fixed," once and for all. I didn't want to have a chronic problem. I didn't want to be someone who fit under the category "depressed" and took "happy pills" to get through the day. I certainly didn't want to be someone who needed medication in order to be myself. Being depressed didn't fit my image of who I was, or what my life was supposed to look like. It made me seem weak and problematic, and suggested that I was responsible for all of my problems, including my unhappy marriage. Admitting I had a chronic health issue was admitting I was inherently flawed, in a way that far exceeded typical "I'm not perfect" admissions.

I never tried to wean myself from anti-depressants again. Since that time, I've been divorced and remarried. My kids are an amazing joy (and not nearly as exhausting as they were a decade ago). The town I didn't want to move to has become a home I wouldn't want to leave—a community populated with friendship and memories, cafes to write in and a church that helped move my faith to a better place. And as the weight of depression lifted, my writing life soared. In addition to my paid freelance work, I started a blog, where I've sorted through so many of my stories—all the ways my life hasn't turned out how I envisioned it, and all the ways God has redeemed it.

But do you know which part of my life was the last to be revealed and grappled with? My depression. And that's something I'm still trying to figure out. I've written a lot about redemption—how it starts with acknowledging the broken pile of scraps in front of you, the pieces that once represented something that seemed beautiful, or could be beautiful. That's where redemption begins, at the scrap heap. With my divorce, it began when I announced to the world that my marriage had failed. We had failed. We were not perfect. We had tried and tried but had decided to give up. It's an incredibly painful but powerful moment—one that triggers all the healing that is poised in the wings, ready to enter the scene.

With depression, I have such a hard time putting the scrap heap on the table. It took me so long to write about it on my blog, and there are still many people I care about who don't know I struggle with depression. It's time to change that, though, because while the antidepressants are important, the real healing still needs to happen. Once the scrap heap is on the table, in full view, it means I'm not only willing to let others see it, I'm in a position to sort through what's there, and see what can be made of it moving forward. That's where the redemption—and the healing—lies: not in being able to get up and walk away from the mess, but in being able, with God's grace, to create something new and beautiful from the contents of that very pile.

Recovery

I remember sitting in the doctor's exam room. I had gone under the guise of needing a physical, which was partially true, but I was mostly there because I knew that I had depression and there was no way that I could get better without some kind of medical intervention.

She came in and we exchanged pleasantries. She did the exam and then asked if there was anything else that I needed. My defenses came down in seconds and with tears dripping down my cheeks, leaving little Rorschach blots on my paper gown, I confessed the struggle with depression that I had been battling for months. I told her that I had dealt with depression before during and after pregnancies, but that in those instances, I had always been able to deal with it by simply talking to people about it. But this time, the wound that had caused my depression was unwilling to heal. It sat there, persistently, day after day, mocking me. It clawed into my brain and sat there, making sure that every aspect of my life was affected by it. And this time, I felt powerless to stop it.

We discussed options available and I decided that in order for talk therapy to work, I needed to take an anti-depressant.

I felt terrible because I was supposed to be able to fix this myself. The words of someone else weren't supposed to have this much of an effect on me. Sure, depression was totally acceptable when I was pregnant or post-partum, but this time? Being hung out to dry by people that I had trusted with my tender heart certainly felt awful, but why wasn't I able to overcome this pain by myself? Why did I need medication to get through this darkness? Sticks and stones and what have you!

But despite my negative feelings, I also knew that there was no shame in taking medication. I knew that there was no single acceptable reason to have depression. And I knew that getting better for my husband, for my children, for my extended family, for my friends, and most importantly, for myself, was what mattered most. Why I was depressed and how I chose to treat that depression were of much lower importance that simply getting well.

The fact is no matter what has caused your depression it is real. And when you come to understand that and accept it, the next step is to decide how you want to treat it.

Seeking help is the first step in recovery. Talking to a trusted friend, a doctor, a counselor, a minister; this is often how recovery begins. Having support and recognizing that I didn't have to go through the darkness by myself helped me sort out what I felt was true (I should be stronger, I should be able to fix myself, someone better than me wouldn't be depressed) from I knew to be true (depression wasn't my fault, it wasn't a moral failing, there is no "right" way to treat it). The medicine helped me order my thoughts so that I was able to separate out the truth from the lie, but without people in my life to encourage me when things seemed dark, the ability to seek help would have seemed nearly impossible.

Like all aspects of depression, recovery is another difficult path to follow. Because depression seems to have as its goal to isolate its victim, finding the courage to seek help is hard. But when you have chosen to accept that you have depression, the only option available is to seek some kind of relief from it. For some, this ends tragically with self-destructive behavior, but for many, including those in the pages to follow, they make different decisions, choices that allow them to live their lives without the constant gloom of depression hanging over them.

Christina, inspired by a behavior chart for her 3 year old niece, found that she needed to make a list of ways that she could check off to make sure she was making positive choices rather than continuing in her destructive habits. Jeremy noticed that when he carved out time for writing, he was able to battle against the demons of depression that threatened to encompass him, reveling in the creative process. Jean found comfort in sea shells, marveling how there is beauty found even in those that are broken and realizing through her faith that God saw her as beautiful and valuable even in her brokenness. And Chuck discovered that the simple act of putting one foot in front of the other lead him from a place of despair to a place of hope.

As you read these stories of recovery, allow them to give you hope that no matter where you are right now, there is no shame in seeking help. There is no embarrassment in taking positive steps toward healing. There is no disgrace in allowing yourself to hope for something different.

~ Alise

22

The Game Of Life

By Christina N. Shumway

Remember playing the board game LIFE as a kid? I was never very good at board games. My younger sister always seemed to beat me. Regardless I always wanted to play after school and LIFE was one of my favorites. The game is simple. You start by picking out your favorite colored plastic car and place your plastic peg-like version of yourself in the driver's seat. With every spin, you gain a career, a spouse, a family, and gifts. You get to play LIFE without having to live with the consequences.

When I turned 18, I realized I wasn't so good at playing real LIFE either. When I landed on typical college age experiences, I was different than those around me. I couldn't seem to "get over" things. Over time my thoughts became darker. It did not matter what anyone said to me. It was my dim reality. All I wanted to do was escape. I wanted so badly to get out of my colored plastic car – only this was not a game, sadly it was my life.

My escape came in many forms. Shopping - check. Eating - check. Purging – check. Sex - check. Partying check, check, and check. Oh and my favorite, sleeping - check. My life seemed like the typical college, 20-something experiencing the "rite of passage", but I always wanted and needed more. The "more" became stronger than my cares for those around me and myself. The cycle of depression and trying to make the pain go away was agonizing and exhilarating all at the same time.

I felt like I was spinning on an emotional hamster wheel. With credit card in hand, I had racked up uncontrollable credit card debt. In four months, my weight went from 193lbs to 115lbs. I found a love for cocaine and prescription pills. And staying out until 6am or not coming home at all became my lifestyle.

I was ready to toss the game board up in the air and end this game of LIFE. I wish I could say I only attempted suicide and over-dosed once, but this was not the case. Sadly, death was such a dark comfort. I felt that suicide was my only option.

My last attempt led me to a psychiatric ward as an involuntary patient. One morning, I was sitting in the small cafeteria. I looked up at the calendar and it was September 11th, 2006. I closed my eyes and remembered where I was on 9-11. I was heading to my chemistry class. It was my senior year of college and I was finishing a semester early. I was graduating with honors. What happened to me? How did I end up in a psychiatric cafeteria? There I sat with a tray of cold tatter tots, stripped of basic daily 'freedoms': not being able to use a pen, having no shoe laces, showering with the door unlocked, and not be able to communicate with others.

My gateway out of the psychiatric ward was an evaluation at a local drug and alcohol rehabilitation center. To my surprise at the time my file read, "inpatient". The average stay in a rehab facility is twenty-one days. But I had determined, "I will not go down without a fight." After forty-two days in sweatpants and three counselors later, the experience started to break me. At this point in my life, I was not crazy about God at all. I did not understand why any God would allow these painful situations to happen in my life. One afternoon, I met with the tall, Dutch chaplain. He asked me, "What do you think about God?" I shared how I wanted nothing to do with a God that would allow those things to happen to me and I certainly was not going to place my trust in Him. He gave a simple response, "God did not allow those things to happen to you." Those words clicked with me. For the first time, I thought about not controlling my own life. I was going to give my life a chance. I went up to my room and wrote down these words on a torn piece of notebook paper, *"God, please hold my hand. I'm scared."* I still have that piece of paper today.

Life didn't magically become better. The life I knew was filled with instant gratification, fulfilling my emotions, wants, and desires. I was in unfamiliar territory. Could I really do this? Just few days after I was discharged from rehab, I was staying at a hotel. It was getting late and I couldn't sleep. My mind was racing which was an all too familiar scenario. Grabbing my new pack of Parliament Lights, I ran out of my room. What I really wanted to do was run from my own thoughts. I lit up a cigarette and broke down in tears. Sitting on the cold sidewalk, I didn't even notice the other patrons passing me by. Eventually I realized a man was knelt beside me. "Are you okay," he said. Hyperventilating I replied, "I'm fine". He was not convinced. As quickly as he stopped, he was gone. His question pulled me out of that moment. I looked down at a now half-empty pack of cigarettes, and I covered my face with my hands. And I just whispered, "God, I need you." I began to say it under my breath over and over and over. The simple four-word prayer of "God, I need you," has become the simplest prayer I say everyday since that cold November night.

I didn't embark upon this journey alone. I began meeting with a counselor named Sarah. She was someone I wanted to be like and I admired her greatly. During our times together, no stone was left unturned. For the first time, I began to reflect on my resentments, fears, and how I had treated others. She listened, challenged, cried, and most importantly spoke truth to me. She didn't take my bullshit. Sarah always told me, "You have a choice. It's yours, but you have to accept the outcome of your choices." One of my biggest challenges was that I enjoyed being a child-like adult. However, I whined that I was not experiencing adult-like rewards. Sarah challenged me to find a job, my own place, and to start paying my bills. If I surrounded myself with adult responsibilities and accountability, I would be placing myself in a lifestyle where it would be difficult to rely on my feelings and emotions.

For two years, I worked full-time (including every weekend) at a local retail store. I made minimum wage, worked with a firecracker of a boss and the general public. Oddly, as I look back I am thankful for that experience. Short on cash and busy with work, I was better equipped to avoid temptations. God was protecting me and showing me His love in ways that I only understand where I stand today. This scripture is one of many that God used to overwhelm me with His love. "Because of the Lord's great love I was not consumed, for His compassion never failed. They were new every morning; great is His faithfulness." (Lam 3:22 – 23 TNIV)

Every day of sobriety brought new and unfamiliar change to my life. I was becoming trustworthy, responsible, independent, and committed. It wasn't just me that noticed the changes, but those closest to me as well. I will never forget the day my mom told me, "Christina, we finally have our daughter back." Or the day my younger sister and brother-in-law approached me about being a

Godmother to their children.

I began to observe simple daily disciplines that helped keep me on track. If I didn't take care of myself emotionally, physically, mentally, and spiritually I knew I would begin to waver. One night while I was babysitting, I noticed a chart on the fridge for my three-year-old niece, Riley. Each day she was rewarded points for good behavior like using the potty, cleaning up her toys, brushing her teeth, or having a good attitude. I decided to apply this same tactic to my life, too. Each day I would conduct my own moral inventory by asking:

- Was I wise with my money?

- Did I take my medications?

- Did I eat well?

- Did I do some sort of physical activity?

- Did I have a good attitude?

- Did I get enough sleep?

- Did I fill my heart today (example: attend church, 12-step meeting, or small group, meditate, volunteer, give to a charity, etc)?

With these questions posted clearly on my fridge, I began to notice how integrated my emotions, body, mind, and spirit truly are. If one is off balance, it affects all other areas of my life.

All seven questions are important, but the one that has brought me so much joy is 'Did I fill my heart today'. A year ago, I noticed that I was becoming very consumed with myself. I was doing all the 'right things', but I was very 'Christina' focused. My local church provides great opportunities and environments for people to grow.

So, I joined a small group, began volunteering once a month, set aside money to give to a charity, organization, or an individual that touched my heart. Those commitments organically spiraled into my daily life. By no means am I Mother Teresa, but I have started to see a change in my heart.

My desire is to have my life and even my past experiences bring hope to others, even if it is just one person. And to be honest, the "game of LIFE" sometimes still sucks. This past week depression hit me hard. A few weeks ago, loved failed me. Reoccurring thoughts of rejection, betrayal, hopelessness, and low self-worth still find their way to me. Sometimes, the pain inside is intense and I want to disappear. Because I have found writing to be so therapeutic, when I find myself in that moment, I pick up my pen and I think of people like you. I don't know if you have lost hope to live or lost trust in humanity. But you are NOT ALONE! I know it hurts, but take courage and choose. Today, choose to love, believe, and forgive even though you do NOT feel like it. And I know with each day, each moment, each hour, we will both get a little bit stronger.

23

The Gaping Chasm of Suicide

By Jeremy Myers

Sometimes I feel that my life is a candle, and the world is a hurricane, threatening to snuff it out. Three years ago, this nearly happened. I lost my job, experienced great financial trouble, and nearly destroyed my marriage. As a result of these events, I entered into a period of deep depression when I felt like all my friends, my extended family, and even God himself, had betrayed me. At times, I wanted nothing more than just to die.

The worst part about losing my job was why I lost it. It was not that I was a bad employee, had done something wrong, or that the organization was downsizing or couldn't pay me anymore. I lost my job because I did what I had been trained to do—research and investigate Scripture and theology. In the course of my research, I began to study some ideas that were on the fringe of what some Christians consider heresy. When my boss found out that I was reading and researching these ideas, he got nervous that I might one day start believing them, and so he took preemptive action, and terminated my employment.

This was a devastating blow. I loved the organization I worked for, the people I worked with, and the future it held for me. Through my work there, I had started to achieve some of my dreams and goals for life. I was breaking into the publishing world, had been a guest speaker at several churches, and had been invited to teach at various conferences. When I lost my job, not only did all of this cease, but nearly all of my friends, acquaintances, coworkers, and even some of my family members, believed the gossip that was being spread, and abandoned or rejected me. As my dreams lay shattered to pieces at my feet, I felt betrayed by all the people in my life, but mostly, I felt betrayed by God.

Yet I still trusted him to do what was right, so I began to do what I had always done in difficult situations: I "took it to the Lord in prayer." But to my horror, things only seemed to get worse. I couldn't find work even though I sent out hundreds of applications. I experienced one financial setback after another. My marriage started to fall apart. At one point, I realized that everything I prayed for turned out exactly the opposite from what I prayed. It was when I stopped praying that things started to improve.

I became angry, bitter, and resentful toward God, and fell into a deep depression. I thought often about how the Scriptures say that "If God is for us, who can be against us?" but in my situation, it should read, "If God is against you, who can be for you?" I understood then how people can become atheists, and why some try to drown their disappointment with alcohol, or deaden their despair with drugs. About three months into this depression, I wrote the following words:

> *There is nothing so fearful as gazing into the glowing eyes of atheism, staggering along the gaping chasm of suicide, or camping near the smoking gates of hell.*

Worse yet, I fear I am here for life. I am never going home. I am never getting out.

Even if I do find my way out of this pit and get back home, I don't have anything left at home to live for. When I began this descent into depression, despair, and doubt, those that didn't stab me in the back as I fell, simply abandoned me. No calls. No e-mails. No letters. Even when I cried out for help, the most frequent response (if I got any response at all) was, "I'll be praying for you." A few told me that this was just a stepping stone to some greater disaster in my life. That was encouraging.

God is playing his part too. It seems like he's up there, just waiting for me to pray, so when I do, he can pounce with delight on my pleading request and crush it. It seems he gives the exact opposite of everything I pray for. When I pray for a fish, he gives me a snake. When I pray for bread, he gives me a rock. I have learned it is better not to pray, because then at least some of what I hope for comes true.

I now understand how people become drug addicts, atheists, and suicidal. My life is over, and each day I live is worse than the day before. I cannot take many more days of this. It might be better to end it all now.

There were other things I wrote—some more hopeful. Some less. The deep depression lasted for about two-and-a-half years. I did end up getting a job, which lasted about three months before I got injured. Then I got another job which provided me a paycheck, but little in the way of satisfaction or fulfillment in life. My wife and I went to marriage counseling. I also started to get counseling for my depression, but often left the office more depressed than when I went in. While I never really considered suicide, I thought often about how nice it would be to get in a fatal car accident, or have some crazy person kill me at work.

The turning point for me was a poem I wrote in late 2010. It was a badly written poem about depression, and I include it below, not because it is good, but because of what happened as a result of writing this poem:

> *Two roads diverged in a wood, and I,*
>
> *I wandered off into the woods, to die.*
>
> *Neither path held hope for me.*
>
> *No hope in life; less for eternity.*
>
>
> *Every decision that led me here,*
>
> *Brought only more pain, shame, and fear.*
>
> *So too fearful to take another step,*
>
> *I lay down in the dirt and wept.*
>
>
> *I hate all those happy, smiley people,*
>
> *Offering empty words from gleaming steeples.*
>
> *And the God they claim to represent?*
>
> *Him I truly do resent.*
>
>
> *When I pray, he does the opposite.*
>
> *I ask for bread; he gives me shit.*

And his Bible? How absurd!

Empty promises; empty words.

If God is not at my side,

It's better to be alone on this ride.

So I shake my fist at an empty sky,

Abandon my kids and leave my wife.

I wander off so I can be alone.

My only companions rock and stone,

I cannot speak, I will not cry;

I just curl up in a ball, and wait to die.

For some strange reason, a poorly written poem about my depression caused a creative spark of life in me. I wrote those words in the midst of my despair, and yet the simple act of writing a poem about my pain and anger reconnected me with a part of my humanity that had lain dormant and unused far too long. That spark of light brought forth hope that maybe my life could rise from the ashes. Maybe the shattered pieces of my life could be put back together again. Maybe resurrection was possible.

The act of writing the poem was an act of healing. It was therapeutic. Looking back now, it seems that my life was without form and void, but the Spirit of God was hovering over the surface of the deep waters of my soul, and into this darkness, God said, "Let there be light." And there was light. A tiny spark of creative power from a poem brought order to the chaos.

As a result of the poem, and though talking with my wife, I realized that writing helped me climb out of depression. Writing helped focus my thoughts, calm my mind, and shed light on my fears. Writing made me feel that God was with me once again. Sometimes when I write, I feel God's pleasure toward me as my fingers dance across the keyboard. I feel hope again. I feel like I am no longer alone.

I doubt that writing will help everyone who faces depression, and I am not sure it will always help me, but it is what helps me right now. So, working with my wife and a counselor, we developed a plan that allows me to spend quality time writing.

The plan doesn't always work, and I have to make sure I don't write at the expense of my family, but the schedule is as follows: I work Wednesday through Sunday, mostly during the afternoons and evenings. My "weekend" is Monday and Tuesday. Unless there are some family activities or errands, I write for about six hours on Monday and Tuesday, and then also for about two hours on Wednesday and Thursday, for a total of sixteen hours per week. To some, this may seem like a lot. And it is, especially when you factor in a full-time job and living life with my wife and children. But to compensate, I have removed other things from my life, which used to consume time: television, video games, Internet surfing, and even reading have been put aside. As much as I enjoyed some of these activities, they did not help with my depression, and sometimes contributed to it.

I have now been in "recovery" for about six months. But just as an alcoholic is always an alcoholic, I doubt I will ever fully recover. I still fall back. I still stumble. Even now, as I remember the pain and fear, which led to my depression, I feel my chest begin to tighten. Panic rises in my thoughts with a fearful sense of doom that I am walking into a trap. I still sometimes feel that most people want to betray me, and that next week, or next month, God will once again crush all my hopes and dreams. It is still difficult to trust anyone at work, to open my soul to my extended family, or to pray honestly to God.

But though I am hopeful, my hope is a tiny flame, which I shield against the hurricane gales of life. That flickering light is my life, for it reveals the gleaming edge of the razor on which I walk, and I know that if a stray gust of wind snuffs it out, I will surely fall back into the chasm, into the pit, which has no bottom. If that happens, I don't think I can climb out again.

So I write. I madly write, as my hand protects the flickering flame against the wind. Sometimes, it seems that the hand protecting the flame is not mine, but God's.

24

Not Just a Girl

By Megg Joosten

I'm not an overly emotional 13-year-old girl (at least not anymore).

What do you think of, when you hear that someone is writing about his or her depression? Often that; the overly emotional teen who thinks no one understands her and no one knows the pain she goes through. Writing out her worries and concerns to the Internet, because no one else cares.

When I write about my depression, it isn't because I believe no one understands me, or because no one knows the pain I go through. That is not why I do it. I write simply because it makes me feel good, and in some small way I want to be able to help someone. However, writing about depression when I'm not feeling depressed is like talking about the bitter cold of winter in the middle of a hot, summer day. It's difficult to properly explain, but it's also not something I want to talk about. Hot as it may be, summer is so fun that no one wants to think about the middle of winter. Even so, I need to try, because it's so important.

Once upon a time I *was* an overly emotional 13-year-old girl. I am going to date myself slightly, but when I was 13 the internet was not what it is today, and there was no outlet for me to cry out to... at least not in the way blogs and online journals are there today. I did keep a journal, however, and in many ways I'm glad I didn't post those thoughts publicly, because they were dark, unhappy, and not something I should be sharing.

A few times, however, I did try to share my thoughts with people. There were a few "mentors," women I really looked up to when I was a teen. They were great sounding blocks, but there was one thing in common with all of them. They brushed my feelings off. Oh, I don't mean they didn't care, far from it. They cared very much for me. They would listen, and nod understandingly, but at the end of the conversation, the outcome was always the same. Whether they said it or not, I now realize that they were simply writing me off as an over emotional teen girl.

I remember one time I read an article in a teen magazine that talked about depression. It had one of those quizzes at the end where you check off symptoms, and if you have 3 or more, you may be depressed and should talk to your doctor. I had several of those symptoms, at the time. The typical depression symptoms: trouble sleeping, lack of interest in activities that used to give you pleasure, weight gain or loss, loss of appetite, etc. However, when I brought this up to my mentor, I was told that those types of articles make everyone feel like they are depressed, and that it didn't mean anything.

I spent *years* depressed, off and on, and had no idea. These things that were told to me in middle school and early high school stuck with me, and I pushed the thought that I may be depressed aside. Now that I look back on it and realize what was happening, I'm shocked and upset, but mostly angry. Angry because I could have fixed this sooner. I didn't have to wait 7 years before I went on medication, or tried to treat my depression on my own.

More often than not, my depression went through phases, times when I was more depressed than others. Often these were set off by then advent of winter. At the time I had no idea how common this is; Seasonal Affective Disorder, or SAD, is very common. The problem for me was that it just never went away. About a year after I started dating my boyfriend (now my husband), the excitement of being in a relationship started to die down. I still loved him, of course, but we were dating long distance and work was busy and stressful. Night after night we talked, but half the conversation I spent in tears for one reason or another. I missed him, I'd picked a fight, he was late in calling...you name it, I cried about it. It wasn't until he mentioned that I might be depressed that I understood what was happening. I felt relieved when I realized that there was a reason for my moods! There was an explanation for my feelings. I made an appointment with my doctor.

I will never forget the day the Prozac she gave me started working. I was house sitting and walking the dog at the time when I realized that I was okay. I felt good for the first time in a year. It was like a veil had been lifted. I was truly happy. It's been almost four years since that day and I still remember the feeling of finally...feeling.

It hasn't always been easy. I've dealt with many different stressful things since then, including the death of a loved one, buying a house and getting married. Since then I also switched medications, to one a little better suited for me. In the process of doing this, however, things got a little rocky again. The process of changing medications was more complicated than I'd anticipated. When I was feeling well it was easy to think the new dosage was working. Thankfully I had a very supportive husband who helped me through the transition until we both were happy with the new medication. I was happy because I wasn't feeling depressed, and he was happy because my crying episodes were limited to just once a month.

One of my favorite songs, The Cave by Mumford and Sons, speaks to me about my depression. The song can mean so many different things, but that's what I hear in it. This song has a line that goes, "So make you siren's call, and sing all you want, I will not hear what you have to say..." Depression calls to me like the friend I know is no good for me that I can't seem to shake. The "siren's call" threatens to pull me down but I refuse to listen. I refuse to let it take hold of my life again. There are times when it slips in, of course. This is why I like to say I struggle with depression. I don't think I will ever be cured. I believe that I will always have to deal with it, but that doesn't mean I need to let it take over.

Everyone has fears of the future. I think most parents fear for their children, whether they have them or not. Will they have a good life? Will they be successful, have good friends, be happy? I worry about these things too, except I worry about one more. I'm completely terrified that these children will become depressed too and have no one to talk to.

I guess this is what I want people to know; this is why I write. I want everyone, no matter their age, to recognize the signs of depression. To know it is not a shameful thing, that it really exists. I want them to listen to their hearts, and not take the advice of misleading but well-meaning friends or mentors. I want them to know they are not alone.

25

The Perfect Storm

by Chad Jones

I've avoided this for far too long--am in fact nearly two months overdue on turning my revised copy in. The fact is, while I would love to have some copy in print—be published as part of a real, honest to goodness book--the thought also terrifies me. It's frightening because it implies that I have to go back to *that* place, relive *those* memories.

I've avoided it by being snarky on the Internet, by hiding behind my humor. By writing other pieces--successful pieces, certainly-- but not what I'm *supposed* to be working on. Which is revising this piece on my bout with depression (like a bad bit of programming, it's something of a recursive loop). I suppose my real fear is that by going *there*, I'll slide down the rabbit hole again.

And that's not a place I want to go.

I consider myself to be a positive person, but I suppose life experiences--a herky-jerky childhood, for one--set me (in addition to brain chemistry) up to fall. Honestly, when life blindsides me with a two-by-four, I crumple. I wish this were not so--I'd like to think I'm getting better--but it is.

Which is why, under the confluence of factors you're about to read of, I went to dark places.

Oh, on the outside I may have been a pleasant enough person, but to those who know me--like my wife--it was an entirely different matter. That inner storm--that "perfect storm"--spilled over in ways both unforeseen and ugly.

It is my hope in sharing the story of depression, you are encouraged to seek hope, help, and community. I hope you come to understand that you are not alone.

~~

It's been at least a couple of years now, but it seems just like yesterday: I had been working away on a piece of long form fiction. In my mind, it was vibrant and living. The characters weren't my creation, but real people. For this reason, though I'd never submitted before, I decided to query an agent, with little to no knowledge of the industry.

The letter (well, email) I got back wasn't harsh, or critical--it was kind in its own form-letter kind of way. In fact, it was the literary equivalent of the infamous "it's not you, it's me" break-up line. Only we were breaking up before even getting a chance to know each other. I put on a brave face, replied to the agency, and thanked them for my first rejection letter. But honestly, it stung more than I was willing to admit.

It would be disingenuous to call a 45-minute daily writing session a river of words--so let's call it a faucet, instead, shall we? Well, that faucet slowed to a trickle. Then dried up altogether.

For some reason, I owned that rejection letter. The agency wasn't rejecting just my work, but me personally. And rejection was just something I was ill equipped to handle. Coming from a broken home, with a very sarcastic, caustic, dad, I'd felt the sting of rejection all of my life. I remember as if it were yesterday, standing under the scorching Phoenix sun in front of the Johnny Bench Batterup my dad installed in our backyard, awaiting his instruction. Trying to follow his directions, trying to please him, with his response to merely throw his hands up and stalk off in frustration, in search of a beer. Apparently, there was something the "hell" wrong with me. That stupid form rejection letter put me in a tailspin, a funk so deep, that I was blocked.

This led me to reengage with some old familiar friends ("besetting sins").

Rather than recite a laundry list of sins here, I can say that the cycle usually begins for me when I catch myself not caring. For instance, I will agree to do, something, and then go do it anyway. And not care one whit about it. Usually this revolves around the accumulation of things—such as books—that I don't need any more of. The "not caring" brings out these latent hoarding tendencies, which precipitates a darker turn when I look at house full of clutter, and don't know where to begin in cleaning it up. It paralyzes me, and I spiral further downward. I lash out with sarcasm, I become sullen and withdrawn, uninterested in the lives of those closest to me, losing care for the quality of my work at my job, eventually not caring about life itself. Wondering whether God should bring me home.

Fortunately for me, God wasn't at all interested in leaving me in that place, and was faithful to clue my wife in. And I'm so thankful she drew her line in the sand, confronted me, and loved me enough to not allow me to continue down a self-destructive path. This allowed some much-needed moments of clarity.

Those times when I was on a more even keel emotionally--akin to trying to balance solo on a teeter-totter--I became increasingly aware that I hadn't felt well physically in quite some time. I had been having nighttime palpitations, bouts of nocturia, and according to my wife, apparent trouble breathing at night during sleep.

So I scheduled a sleep study--which determined that I had sleep apnea (an airway obstruction, which causes one's body to stop breathing during sleep; consequently, the body wakes itself up enough to start breathing again. The net result of which is one doesn't rest), for which I was prescribed an assistive breathing (CPAP) device. And for my palpitations, the doctor put me on Atenolol (a beta blocker). These seemed to work. I wasn't feeling great, but somewhat better, I guess.

But the Atenolol had a particular side effect, which for someone of my--or any--age, was rather disconcerting. So back to the doctor I went. I even changed doctors. Had more extensive testing, including the glorious 24-hour urine collection (if this is on your list of things to do before Jesus returns, cross it off! I've done it, and it sucks!).

Turns out, my blood pressure was fine--but my Thyroid wasn't. All this time, I'd had undiagnosed Thyroid disease!

It was the hypothyroidism that had precipitated my:

- Sleep apnea
- Heart palpitations
- Wait gain
- Lack of energy
- And...My depression

My own body chemistry worked against me; around the same time I got that rejection letter, to create a perfect storm of ick. Which took me tumbling down into the depths. These depths included: withdrawal from my wife and kids, not caring about the value of my "word" when given, sarcasm and cutting humor (usually at another's expense), believing lies about myself and those around me. Needless to say, this impacted my outlook—blue skies were always gray. The impact to my marriage was an overwhelming disconnect between my wife and I, and a laissez faire attitude towards parenting my children. Nothing mattered more than getting whatever "dope" I thought I needed to make myself feel better about me. While none of it involved illicit substances, none of it was healthy. And my wife knew, as they do, that I was keeping secrets. And I didn't care.

I'm still not 100%, but more in tune with my body, more aware of my symptoms. There are still mornings when I awake—exhausted— wondering why God hates me. These are fewer, but still happen. In my heart, I know he doesn't hate me, but when I open my tired eyes to greet another day, sometimes I wonder. I still use a CPAP, and get about 4-6 hours of sleep per night. It may not be great rest, but thank God I'm alive! I will be on supplemental Thyroid hormone for the rest of my life. Since I've begun blogging regularly, I've discovered— through reading blogs like Anne Jackson's, Alise Wright's, and others—that I'm not alone. The honesty and transparency these people display day in and day out has encouraged me to go public with my struggles. In so doing I've discovered that I'm truly not alone—there are people out there who can identify with where I'm at. And the cliché is true: confession is good for the soul. The biggest lie of my depression was the isolation, that I was alone in it. Now I know better, and am armed against it.

Thank-you for reading! May God bless you as you reach for healing and wholeness. You are not alone!

26

Getting Out of the Pit

By Joe Sewell

For all we know about it today, depression remains stigmatized by society, especially the one place where safety should be found: **the church**. So many people don't realize that depression may very well be "just in your head," but that it's a real **medical** condition, at least for some of us.

I've been diagnosed with, and treated for, a serotonin imbalance. This means, in essence, that much of my depression and anxiety is outside of my mental control. I can't "think it away" with "positive thoughts" or excitement. In fact, excitement can often trigger panic and anxiety attacks, which are related. The beginning of my recovery might be disappointing for some hoping for a miracle. I went on an antidepressant and a tranquilizer, taken as needed, for those times when I get out of control. That may seem boring, even undesirable to some, but for me it **was** a miracle.

The medications remove one of the barriers to my healing: whatever glandular defects are involved that inhibits either the production or proper usage of serotonin. Yes, that's how I treat the physiological part of my depression, as a physical defect. No, that doesn't mean God made a mistake, any more than He did when someone is born without arms or legs, or with Type 1 diabetes. I look at the medications as a Type 1 diabetic looks at insulin: it's medically necessary for my survival.

The psychological part of it has been a different story. No, you really can't tell what aspects of your depression are purely from the serotonin issues and what aspects are psychological results of the physical. I'm no psychiatrist or psychologist, but I haven't been able to distinguish between the two. Both feed on each other. Hurt compounds on hurt, anxiety upon anxiety, excuse for depression upon excuse.

You read that correctly. I called it an excuse. In Christ there really is no excuse for depression outside of the physical. That's not saying recovery is easy, especially if you've dealt with the physical issues for years before getting treatment. It took over 30 years for me to be diagnosed officially with depression, but it was the same moment that I learned of the physical side of it. As the physical side is overcome, it's time to start believing the promises found in God's Word, such as there being no condemnation in Christ (Romans 8:1) or that nothing can separate us from His love (Romans 8:31-39 … I suggest The Living Bible, if you can find it, for this particular passage).

Recovery takes time. I hesitated putting this into the "Recovery" category because I haven't completely recovered yet. I still get depressed. I'm still afraid of getting depressed. Part of recovery, though, is in realizing that some amount of depression is normal … whatever that means in our world today. Part of recovery is in **balancing** depression with the knowledge that God loves us literally to death (John 3:16). How can somebody be depressed when you're that blessed? I hate to say this, but it's too easy for some of us. It seems that depression can be just as much of a "habit" as anything else we think, say, or do. Those of us who have experienced clinical depression have a hard time comprehending just how to feel joy. Even after being diagnosed with it over 10 years ago, it's still hard to imagine not experiencing ongoing feelings of sadness.

As I turn to God in prayer, though, He reminds me of what my life has been worth to others. There's a young boy living with his mommy right now that is alive because of me. The mother had just turned 18, and became pregnant. She was afraid of her parents finding out, afraid that they would kick her out of her home. Rather than admit what happened, she was ready to have an abortion. I told my wife to talk her out of it while I rushed to a pay phone (this was just before cell phones had almost replaced those icons) to look up the phone number of the local Pregnancy Resources Center. We told her that we had a spare room that was hers if she did get kicked out. We told her we were truly there for her no matter what. We encouraged her to keep the baby. The young fellow is approaching the age of 6 now, and his mother reminds us that he's here because of us ... because of **me**!

The Spirit of Christ still brings that to mind. At first I would respond by saying if I hadn't been there, say because I had taken my own life earlier, God would've provided somebody else. I would especially think that when I'd imagine never having existed at all. (For the record, I've never watched the movie It's A Wonderful Life. In my depression I'd deny that such a series of events would ever happen with me.)

The Holy Spirit's response to me is puzzling. He says to me that if I hadn't been around to help that mommy-to-be, He could have used somebody else, but then that person wouldn't have been able to do what he or she was doing for the Kingdom of God at that moment, which would have required rerouting someone else, which would have left a "gap" there, which would have required someone else to step in there, and so forth and so on. I could almost hear the God of Abraham, Isaac, and Jacob say, "*Oy vey!* What a mess that would've made." (That's silly, of course. I mean, where in the King James Version does God not sound like Charlton Heston?)

The point is made, though. I was there because that's where God wanted me! I was there to save that boy's life and that mother from the horror of abortion! To this day that young mother reminds me how grateful she is that we were there for her when she needed Christ in us. She has also recommitted her life to the Lord.

The thought that I made a positive difference that somebody else couldn't have is still difficult for me to comprehend, let alone accept. There it is, though. The guy who is afraid of being around kids for a variety of reasons, many of which stem from the depression and anxiety that have been present for so long, is responsible for "saving" a child's life and a mother's sanity and soul! **How can I stay depressed with that thought for very long?**

Perhaps that's what recovery is all about. Perhaps recovery isn't necessarily a miraculous instantaneous healing and freedom from all depression and anxiety. Perhaps recovery is in having the courage to admit that I don't know it all, that the thoughts depression brings to mind from time to time aren't valid, aren't true, and definitely aren't what my heavenly Father think of me. Perhaps recovery is dealing with the memories of how members of my own family and circle of peers put me down, how I believed those put-downs, but now chose to view my life through the eyes of God's unshakeable love. Perhaps recovery means continuing to battle depression and anxiety as my own version of the apostle Paul's "thorn in the flesh" (2 Corinthians

12:5-10), reminding myself that I'm not unworthy because I didn't receive immediate healing, that the love of God is not dependent on my being healed, but rather that I can write for projects like this one, staying in the war to lead people out.

Maybe you who are reading this are still caught in depression. Maybe you want to "abort" in your own way. I've been there 3 times, twice since surrendering my life to Jesus. The first was at the age of 10. I felt like my life was a waste of space on this planet. I had no idea that a young girl, with a young man forming inside her, were depending on me not pulling that trigger, or walking into the ocean to drown, or driving my car off a bridge, or whatever other way I've thought of bringing my unbearable life to an end, bringing my **fear** of life to an end. You've got someone depending on you, too. You probably won't know who it is right now. Perhaps you do know. Perhaps recovery is making one little decision, right now, to believe that maybe, just maybe, there's a life waiting for **you, and you alone**, to come to his rescue.

Perhaps recovery is trusting that God knows what He's doing, and persevering in spite of the depression, even when life seems to hurt so much. Perhaps feeling that pain is part of the recovery. Perhaps you need to find out for yourself, and then write your own story as I've just done, so someone else can learn how to recover.

27

Blindsided

By Dana McCoy

Have you ever been blindsided by something in your life thinking, "It could never happen to me?" I think that is how depression starts, perhaps it's because something happens in our life that we never expected and we don't know how to deal with it. I'd gone to church all my life and never really had any problems but all that changed and I found myself in a pit.

In Jeremiah 29:11 - NIV we read," For I know the plans I have for you, declares the Lord, plans to prosper you and not to harm you, plans to give you a hope and a future."

Do you really believe that verse, or are you like me when I say, "God, this is my plan, I submit it to you for your approval." I say I trust God with all that's going on in my life, but I think that I can control my circumstances. I chalk that up to my personality, or the way I grew up. My father had always been in charge, in control, and I was a lot like him. Several things happened in my life to convince me that this verse was really meant to bring me comfort and to help me realize that God's plan is really best for my life, so I'd better start listening to Him.

My husband and I had been married 27 years, had 3 wonderful daughters. Like most families, I was a working wife and mother and our life was busy and active. We attended school functions with our daughters, were actively involved with our church and had a music ministry taking God's word on the road. We appeared to be very happy to everyone who knew us, and we believed that we were happy, but like most families, there were a few potholes in the road of our lives. When things would go wrong, we would either apply a little hot patch to get over the problem, or just drive around it to avoid hitting that hole, that somehow never got fixed.

Like many couples, we lived separate lives. As a teacher, my husband found many extracurricular jobs to be involved in. As advisor for the yearbook and the newspaper, there were constant reasons to stay at work late, or go back to work to take pictures, attending a sporting event or concert. What first attracted me to him was his unique talent. We met in a musical in college and fortunately, I'd never heard anyone say that there was no such thing as love at first sight. There was for me, I just had to convince him. Because of his dramatic flair, he assisted with musicals at the high school for several years and could have continued this indefinitely, but found that the stress of working with so many personalities just wasn't for him. I pursued my individual interests by spending more time at work, or participating in my favorite hobby, shopping. With 3 daughters, it was easy to find something to do with each of them to take me away from being at home.

You could probably say that we knew there was something wrong with this life style and we attended several marriage conferences to find out how to fix it, but they all seemed to come up short. I don't think we really wanted to fix it, because we'd have to change, to give up our own desires and look for God's plan for us as a couple.

As I just said, my husband is very talented and was asked by our pastor and some friends at church if he would be involved in a Christian community dramatic production. We had an empty nest, with no high school events involving our children to attend, so we both thought that this would be a good idea. As a full time department manager at work, I thought I'd enjoy an evening alone and encouraged my husband to use his talents. Things seemed fine until the month before production. It was amazing to me how long rehearsals lasted and I thought that his after school hours seemed to be longer as well.

Have you ever said, "It could never happen to me?" That's exactly what I thought until I found a card from another woman in my husband's van. My life crumbled right before my eyes. He assured me that it meant nothing to him and that he had no intention of seeing her again. She was just a friend from the production, but the card wasn't one that you'd get from a friend. Knowing that it couldn't happen to me, I believed him and tried to continue life as if nothing had happened, because I knew that nothing had, but there was a tension between us that nothing could erase.

The summer of '99 was a difficult one for me because we had 2 daughters out the country. Our middle daughter was studying opera in Italy while our youngest was on a mission trip with Campus Crusade in Africa. Our life centered on phone calls at strange hours or hoping for an email that things were fine. I worked every day, but as a teacher my husband had the summer off. It was a happy 4th of July in '99 because that was the day our youngest returned home. Our house was decorated with a welcome home banner while our driveway was lined with American flags. Little did I know that such a reunion would be shattered 11 days later when I realized that my husband was still seeing this other woman.

Did I mention God's plan? He knew that our youngest was extremely strong after the persecution she had witnessed in a Muslim nation. Perhaps that is why when I questioned my husband regarding some evidence that I had found, he confessed. Just as in Luke 22:31 - NIV Jesus said to Peter "Satan has asked to sift you as wheat," our family was being sifted. Would we remain faithful, or succumb to the temptation. I was living with someone I hardly knew for the past 5 months, but God's plan was that I would be ministered to and comforted by my youngest daughter. She prayed while we went to church at 10PM to meet with our pastor. Our pastor counseled my husband to call the other woman and end their relationship at that time, but he refused. The next morning we went back for another meeting and at this time he decided that he would make the phone call. Several days later we met with the other couple and forgiveness was asked for and granted by both offending parties.

Why do I tell you this story? To let you know that there is hope. The most devastating loss that can occur is the loss of hope. Satan chooses to tempt those who have the most to lose, but God is stronger and can change our circumstances if we will cry out to Him. My husband was not unfaithful sexually, but he was emotionally absent from our marriage. It was difficult for him to say no to a relationship where someone was constantly telling him how talented he was, how much he was needed, and since they were both Christians surely this couldn't be wrong. In Jeremiah 29:11 – NIV God's promise is not for health, wealth, or fame, but for hope. "I will give you a hope and a future." Our problem is that we want to know what that future is right now.

When we encounter problems in our lives it may be because God is trying to teach us something, but most of the time we are so busy with our own agenda that we fail to see the lesson that He is trying to teach us. God calls us to forgive as we have been forgiven. When our problems were revealed to our family members, we praised God that they all were in an attitude of forgiveness and that our marriage had withstood the test of time and temptation.

This happened 12 years ago and I have often had trust issues, but then I am reminded that only God can fill my greatest needs and I have also let people down. I continue to be married to the same wonderful, talented man that I met all those years ago and know that it is for life.

I had questioned my significance for years, especially after the betrayal. I felt I was ordinary and had no special talents. My husband was an actor and could always stand out in a crowd because of his talents. When I was a child and teenager, my mother thought she was protecting me by saying, "You can't do that" or "You don't want to try that". She thought that never trying meant never failing. I had successes in my life and with my family but it wasn't until I realized that my significance was in Christ and what He did for me that I knew it wasn't about what others thought of me but that God loved me and sent Hi one and only Son for me. I feel the Lord gave me these words of encouragement, to give me hope and remind me of His love for me.

One day while walking along the shore at Edisto Island, I was impressed by how different each seashell was. The difference in size, color and shape made me reflect on the different experiences I've had in my life.

The white shells reminded me of the bright spots in my life: my graduation, my wedding day, as well as the birth of my children and grandchildren.

The dark shells brought to mind the difficult times I've had to endure: the loss of a loved one, a broken relationship, and the ordinary stress of day-to-day life.

But the shells I like the best are the broken ones.   These made me think about the pieces of my life.   As I look at these pieces, I can hear my Lord say, "You're broken my child, but without this brokenness you can't grow.   As you let me comfort you, you will learn to comfort others.   I love you so much that I sent my one and only Son, Jesus to die for you."

Just like I went looking for these shells and collected them so God came looking for me.   He calls me by name and promises that He will never leave me or forsake me.   What a joy and what a simple lesson to be learned from a few ordinary sea shells, each one different, each one special, just like each one of us is special to our Heavenly Father when we seek a relationship with Him.

I pray that you will be reminded of how special you are to God.   It's not about our position in life or our possessions, but just about how much He cares.   He calls you by name, too, and promises that He won't leave you either.   When the creator of the universe says that, how can we doubt our purpose and significance?

I started out by saying that I was blindsided however I found out that I was blindsided by God's love in a way that I had never experienced before.   He is the reason that I have a truly healthy marriage now because we both looked to Him for our strength and significance.

28

Redemptive Suffering

By Kyla Cofer

I'm of the mindset that depression, like cancer, is a disease. One that you can do things to prevent but sometimes it just happens. A friend of mine underwent two brain surgeries for a cancerous tumor. When he received the cancerous diagnosis, he told everyone he knew. My friend asked people to support him, and consistently updated his community on his recovery progress. Never once did he feel shame for having a destructive brain tumor; never once did his friends and families blame him for the disease. The cancer was accepted as a disease – something that happened *to* him, not something that he asked for. While a person can take steps throughout their life to prevent cancer, sometimes it seeks out healthy and unsuspecting individuals. Cancer starts small, and left untreated, it wreaks havoc on the body.

Once depression, like cancer, invades your body, you must actively do something to get it out. For some, medication is required. For others, healthy eating, exercise, and a full social calendar will do the trick. Still for others, years of counseling, prayer, and a combination of all of the above will fight the battles of depression. This essay is not about the scientific studies behind depression, nor is it about finding a place of agreement about depression. The purpose of my writing is this: to break the stigma behind the disease as well as to offer a little more vulnerability into my own life for those who wish to know it.

Yesterday, as I sat in my office fighting back tears, the following thoughts played through my mind:

> *"I'm not good enough."*
>
> *"I'll never get this right."*
>
> *"I'll never get married. (Aka: no one wants me)"*
>
> *"I'm lazy."*
>
> *"I should walk away."*
>
> *"What's the point?"*
>
> *"I'm tired."*
>
> *"I have no motivation."*
>
> *"I shouldn't be the one to do this."*
>
> *"I'm the black sheep, and no one will ever see things the way I do."*
>
> *"I'm going to fail."*

Thankfully, many years of battling depression have taught me a few things. The above thoughts were intermingled with:

"Those are lies."

> *"Satan wants me to fail."*
>
> *"God wants to love me."*
>
> *"You are what you eat. I've spent an entire month eating*

*anything but healthy foods, this physically affects the
way my mind operates - time to get healthy."*

*"Oh yeah, I haven't exercised much lately, either. Who
wants to join me for a 5 mile run this weekend?"*

*"While I love my family and they love me, we don't
always treat each other the best. We also don't do such
a great job at respecting each other's differences. That
takes radical grace, and I'm not so good at it. After a
week of "vacation" with my entire family, I'm weary of
my internal battles and simply need to rest."*

"It's alright to cry, it might make me feel better."

*"I have a steady community, who loves me heaps. It's
okay to admit to them that I don't have it all together. I
can stop being so damn independent."*

*"This will pass; it's just difficult in this moment. Life
is difficult, there are always challenges, but I have
overcome them before and I will again. The Holy Spirit
fights these battles with me."*

*"I'm always being offered a new way to see things. Will
I choose to see?"*

I went for a walk at lunch and saw the sun. I focused myself on the
present moment that I can do something about; instead of looking
towards things I have no control over (the past). I remembered the
gifts that I've been given and the way love has been showered onto
me. I accepted how I was feeling, and then chose not to wallow in
it. I decided that if I needed to, I would take medication again. I
checked out Ecounseling.com for some encouragement, and read
several encouraging blog posts. I made plans so that I wouldn't be
stressed about the things I needed to accomplish. I spent the evening

with my awesome community to celebrate a birthday. Celebrations are important - they remind us of hope and joy in life. I listened to my friends talk about how we have intentionally chosen to be friends, and share life together (my spirit heard: someone wants you!) I laughed ridiculously at the pranks they've played, met new people, shared my sadness, and enjoyed the present.

There are friends who I've spoken with over the last few months who are full to the brim with hurts and sorrow. It might be time to empty that pitcher of dirty water and fill it with fresh, living water. Just like taking chemotherapy to destroy cancer, you have to actively work to destroy depression. There will be something that works for you, whether through healing prayer, medication, raw foods, volunteering, or running a marathon.

There is a time for mourning and grief, absolutely. Hurt and sorrow should never, ever, be ignored or downplayed. Emotional pain is legitimate and must be given its place in life. If you remember anything I wrote here, remember this: that there is a love that redeems all suffering, a love that is compassionate in our suffering and waits with us through it.

Your suffering and pain are real.

Your suffering and pain are not being ignored.

Your suffering and pain will be redeemed, not revenged.

You may see suffering and pain again in your lifetime.

Your suffering and pain require great things of you. They require that you hope. They require that you love. They require humility. They require grace. They require honesty. They require compassion, community, and solidarity.

When your suffering and pain turn to abundant peace and hope, there will be great rejoicing.

If you are feeling discouraged today, seek out someone who will give you personal encouragement and who can connect you with other resources. If you have one friend, tell them why your heart is hurting, and resolve to be a participant in your healing. Find a reason to celebrate.

29

Getting Better: Running to Find Myself

By Chuck Larish

Mile 1

I stepped onto the front porch in my sweat pants and slightly tight T-shirt that clung uncomfortably to my pudgy torso. It was unseasonably warm outside for an October afternoon. The sun was out, the sky was blue, and it was a gorgeous day. And I felt worse than I'd ever felt in my entire life. I stepped off the porch and set my foot to the pavement for the first time in over 15 years, determined to run as far and as fast as I could. If I couldn't run from my problems metaphorically, I'd run from them physically and in the process, hopefully do something good for myself. Hopefully. As I took my first stiff steps down the sidewalk, I let my mind wander in an attempt to recover.

I couldn't believe it. The worst-case scenario I had imagined had just come true. I had no job, no career, no prospects, no goals, and no dreams for the future. How could this have happened? The previous year, I had been a teacher, directing a music technology program at a community college, and just two years earlier in 2008, I'd been a brand new dad with a five-month-old son in an audio production career that I loved with a job that I didn't but was decent enough. When I left my position at the college in May 2010, I was sure that I had a new gig at Big Toy Company, and that my triumphant return to professional audio production was waiting for me. My career had been progressing rapidly but now there was nothing but silence.

The last major hit I took, my failed application to Big Toy Company, simply crushed the little hope I had left and blew it away in a single puff of stilted breath. Through the first half of 2010, I progressed easily through their application process knowing that I was going to quit my teaching gig at the college no matter what happened. I had great phone interviews. I was flown out for a personal interview. I heard positive feedback from the interviewers. Contrary to my usual practice, I let myself believe in myself, that I had a chance at obtaining my goals. But when their deadline for a decision came and went and again all I heard was silence, my stomach dropped. I knew that I was not getting the job despite all the energy, hope, care, and love that had I poured into my application. It was frustrating at the least, infuriating at the worst. My life was on hold and since I'd already quit my teaching job there was nothing left.

The point at which my career disappeared in a single mirror-smashing moment of shattered dreams was when I stumbled. I fell headlong into a major bout of depression, deeper than I'd felt in a long time. As a surprised and stunned stay-at-home dad, my son kept me busy, but I still had a very difficult time focusing on anything that may have needed to be done around the house. I would often catch myself staring into space or in my own little daydream world. Day after day, I would wake up before he would call for me from his crib, my head heavy on my pillow and dreaming of leaving, of disappearing, thinking only of the life I could potentially lead and nothing of the one I would be leaving behind. I hid these thoughts from my wife and family. But the day I lost control, the same day I yelled at my son for no good reason and began uncontrollably wailing and sobbing on the basement floor, was the last straw. I couldn't hide this anymore and I couldn't avoid my responsibility to demonstrate maturity and respect to my son. I revealed my issues to my wife and she encouraged me to seek help through counseling.

Mile 2

My feet pounded the pavement quickly with comfortable repetition. The first leg of my inaugural running route was initially downhill. It felt good to move again, to sweat, to feel the warm fall breeze on my arms and face. The smell of the season, a swirling mix of decaying leaves and freshly cut grass, was a gentle perfume to my nose, as my breaths grew increasingly heavy. Having not run for so long, I felt like I was relearning to breathe. I had been out of shape so long that I'd forgotten what it was like to feel the heady rush of endorphins that running could create. As I began to feel better, I continued to recount my recent experiences that led to my current state.

I began seeing a counselor in August. My counselor had told me that not being able to hold a steady job was a red flag for bipolar disorder. But I'd stayed in some very crappy jobs, like the job in the shipping department at a media warehouse, for more than 18 months and most of my jobs were left behind for either good reasons or reasons out of my control. Cable modem installer? Laid off. Data entry for a mortgage lender? I had quit to go to graduate school. How could going back to school be a symptom of bipolar disorder? But there were other symptoms that shed more light on the problem such as racing thoughts almost my entire adult life, especially at night. I would awaken and my mind would refuse to shut down, racing through either good ideas or bad memories depending on my current mood. Spending sprees or simply urges to shop, mild though they might have been, were a common theme. Wanting to cry and to feel sad, coupled with feelings of hopelessness, was also a regular occurrence. Suicidal thoughts, though actual attempts had always been absent, were yet another issue that remained uninvestigated.

Another issue was unearthed during my counseling sessions in addition to the bipolar diagnosis, one that I suspected but always wrote off as being a fad, a pseudo-psychological issue, thanks to popular culture in the 1990s. Since my childhood years, my self-esteem had always been a struggle. Being a common target of bullying in my neighborhood and school growing up probably did not improve my chances of a good self-image, but I chose to listen to the bullies rather than ignore them. Misguidedly taking the bullies' barbs as truth was nothing but a mistake. As an adult, even people that barely knew me had the insight to tell me, "You're being too hard on yourself." I would constantly call myself stupid, un-talented, or just plain useless on a regular basis, verbally punching myself in the face every chance I got.

Mile 3

Finally my hustling, burning feet brought me to the bottom of the hill, sweating, panting, but still feeling energized. If I was going to make it home there was nowhere left to go but up. A long climb lay ahead of me and I stared up at the top of the hill already tired but knowing I could make it if I tried hard enough. I had always been self-conscious about my body image, worried that people would make fun of me from the relative comfort of their cars or homes. I put all of my unreasonable fears aside. If they were going to make fun of me, so be it. I needed to do this for myself. For my wife. For my son. I kept running, shins hurting, out of breath, up the hill as car after car revved past.

Several weeks of counseling were devoted to exploring useful tools I could use to improve myself behaviorally. One major step was correcting my self-esteem, which had always been in the proverbial toilet. To correct this is a day-to-day, sometimes moment-to-moment battle. But a psychologist named Albert Ellis developed a therapy dubbed Rational Emotive Behavior Therapy (REBT) that has seemed to work for me. Whenever I have a negative thought about myself, before those thoughts propagate and snowball in my mind, I must insert a corrective question, a self-checker, that challenges the statement I am making about myself. For instance, before I finish the thought, "I am a useless person because I am unemployed," I must insert a question or a challenge, "Why? How?" and ask myself if what I'm thinking is rational. If it isn't, I must discard the idea. It's a challenging thing to try to reverse a lifetime of thought patterns, but with the help of this system I am starting to succeed.

As for the bipolar bit of the equation, I have been on medication to treat both mood swings and depression for a combination of two months. It seems to be working quite well. In conjunction with the general consensus among the mental health professional community, my most effective path to success has been through a combination of talk therapy and medication. I don't want to stay on medication forever, but I must stick with my doctor's recommendations if I am going to lead a normal and effective life.

But there is one final piece of the puzzle, a prescription that I have given myself, that has done more good than I have ever imagined.

I stuck with the running and added yoga and lifting weights to the mix as well. I now run at least three days a week and I am over half way through a program called Couch to 5k, designed to get inactive people onto their feet and running 3.1 miles in nine weeks. I even purchased new shoes recently, ones designed solely for running. Athleticism has long avoided my attention throughout my life, but I am now deadly serious about running my first 5k. I have a goal for the first time in almost a year. The exercise seems to be doing my brain and my body more good than all of the other therapies put together.

Mile 3.1

Gasping for air, I made it up that hill. It wasn't pretty by any means. It was ugly, sweaty, painful, and to use an understatement, unpleasant. My shin splints were killing me. I slogged the rest of the short distance home until I arrived in my own driveway. Staggering in a circle trying to cool down, I felt something I hadn't felt in a long time: accomplishment. I had forgotten all about the people that might make fun of me. I had forgotten about all the loss and sadness that I felt. My only goal had been to run home. And I had done it. The greatest part of the entire experience was, however, knowing that if I had done it once that I could do it again and through practice, get better.

~~

If you are like me, you've gone your whole life believing that your state of mind is simply what it is and can only be endured, not helped. I am not the first and will not be the last to say that if you experience any symptoms of depression or other related mental disorders, please see a doctor, counselor, or psychiatrist that can get you the help that you need. An exercise regime, while incredibly valuable, is only a single tool among many that needs to be utilized in the process to better your mental health and above all, *get better*.

A Small Update

About four months after I wrote this piece, my psychiatrist removed my bipolar diagnosis. Major depression was still a part of it, but the change allowed me to stop taking certain medications. Following the removal of the bipolar medication, still with the help of my psychiatrist, I was slowly weaned from all of medications and I am now feeling better and drug-free. I continue to use REBT techniques to improve my self-esteem issues.

Post-Depression Reflections

I'm not one who is prone to silence. Anyone who knows me will tell you that I have a loud voice, a louder laugh and no lack of words.

Depression wanted to silence me.

It wanted to make me feel like my voice was not valuable and that my thoughts were simply those of one crazy woman. It tried to steal my laughter by making me focus solely on the negative aspects of my life. It tried to stifle me, to box me in, to leave me feeling isolated.

And for during different seasons during my life, it was successful. I tucked myself away and silenced my voice. I didn't write. I didn't play music. I didn't create. Depression was running the show and depression doesn't want anyone to recognize their value. Depression wants only for you to focus on your faults, real or imagined. Depression wants you to feel small, insignificant, and alone. And it's very good at that.

In the midst of my depression, everything negative was amplified. Tiredness became exhaustion. Anger became rage. Sadness became anguish. Pain became agony. It pressed in and made me hurt, physically, spiritually, physically. It felt inescapable.

But I was able to find an escape.

One day, when I could sense depression settling in, threatening to silence me again, I logged into my blog and wrote a short post.

I told the few people who were reading that I was hurting. That depression had moved from the wings and was making its way to center stage. The post wasn't particularly well written or profound. It was just a note, a bit of code throw out onto the Internet saying, "Hey! I'm struggling!" But the act of writing it was a way for me to stick my tongue out at depression and let it know that this time I wasn't going to let it keep me quiet. I wasn't going to allow it to me feel like a lesser person.

That act of defiance was noted. Other people contacted me to let me know that they too had been in that dark place. They shared their stories. They talked about what they had dealt with or what a loved one had experienced. There was encouragement. There was hope. There was community.

Depression's most powerful tool is that of isolation, and when I cut those legs out from under it, depression had no choice but to retreat.

This isn't to say that depression has forever been vanquished from my life. Maybe, but I doubt it. I've gone rounds with depression in the past and while it has left for periods of time, it has never left entirely. It's there, waiting to make its move. Part of overcoming for me is less about never suffering it again, but finding ways to make episodes shorter and less severe. I have found that when I am open with my struggles, the community that is available to offer support makes that easier to accomplish.

I also discovered that as I invited others to share their stories, hope arose. Hope for me, hope for the writers, and hope for the readers. People who had never come forward about their depression wrote and said those words aloud for the first time. Souls were laid bare and in the midst of the pain, healing took place. We weren't interested in a cure, but we found peace. And in the midst of depression, peace is a precious commodity.

In this final section, the authors look back on depression. How it has affected their lives and how they worked to overcome it in their lives. Melissa shares how her life was defined by her illness, but when she chose to see her intrinsic worth as a person, she was able to shift her focus away from simply existing into a life of value. Leigh shares about the differences that she has been able to find between depression and grief and talks about how important it is for her to distinguish between the two. Allison talks about how disjointed things seem when she has suffered depression and how being on the other side allows her to see the bigger picture. And Tamara exposes the lies that depression whispers and encourages her and us to ignore them and live in the truth.

Thank you for coming on this journey with us. By reading, you have become a part of this community. You have shared in the pain, the hurt, the despair, but you have also shared in the hope. I invite you to walk this last bit with us, so that none need make this journey alone.

~ Alise

30

A Girl's Journey with Depression

By Melissa Binstock

I remember those dark times well, those days of perpetual night and unremitting cold. Yes, I remember them; they were the days of my depression. I was not a typical child. I did not fit into that neat cookie-cutter mold. Instead, I was a misfit child—a child with so many disorders that my diagnostic axis was completely filled. Tourette's syndrome, dyslexia, OCD, ADHD, GAD, anorexia nervosa: these disorders became my labels; these disorders became my identity.

By the time I was 15, I could add a new label to my person—depression. The depression arose largely because of my feeling of being consumed by my disorders. With a Sick Person yelling in my ear every time I tried to eat and a body and mind that refused to cooperate, I felt as though I had no control over myself or my life. The loss of control left me feeling hollow, empty, and utterly consumed by sadness so sickening it sent me searching for some sort of relief.

I turned to cutting myself so that I could feel the pain. Pain, to me, became an easier companion than sadness. I began to actively seek pain so that I could avoid the sadness, the emptiness, and the hollowness. My bathroom became almost like a sanctuary where I would perform my carefully planned cutting rituals, cutting just enough to feel the pain and see the blood but not enough for people to catch on to what I was doing.

In addition to cutting, I also began making myself throw up. Purging became another sort of release for me; a way to purify myself of the toxic feelings of sadness pent up within me. More than anything, though, purging became a new source of pain I could consume myself with so that I wouldn't have to feel the sadness.

There came a point, though, that my sadness became too overwhelming, too all consuming to subdue through pain or distraction; there came a point at which I wanted to end it all. Perhaps I would have too, if it hadn't been for my parents. We had gotten into an argument about some trivial matter. It was as though that argument was the last drop of water needed for a levy to finally burst. And, it did burst. As my mother screamed and my father yelled, I fumbled through the kitchen drawer and grabbed a knife in my violently trembling hand. In front of my parents' eyes, I took that cold blade and thrust it into the skin on my arm, not stopping until the blood ran freely down my arm and onto the marble counter top with a splash. In that moment, I wanted to end it all—I wanted to die.

Yet, there was something about my mother's tears and my father's cries that made me stop and throw down that knife. At that moment, I realized that if I died, I would be hurting more than myself—I would be hurting the people who brought me into the world, who raised me, and who loved me. For the moment, I felt as though I owed it to them to live on. It wasn't until much later that

I discovered that I owed it to myself to continue my life.

Two days after the knife incident, I finally agreed to go to a treatment center to get help. For four months, I was loaded up on food and Prozac, and my mood finally stabilized. I thought I had been cured of the depression; I thought I was finally going to be happy. Yet, when I came home, those same feelings of darkness began to creep up on me. I fought them, tried to subdue them. And yet, they came. Again, I returned to the cycle of restricting, purging, and cutting. Again, I tried to subdue the sadness through pain. Yet, as before, the pain could only suppress the sadness for a time. Something needed to change. And, something did change. I was once again on the brink of giving up hope when my parents stepped in. This time, they saved me by introducing horses back into my life.

When I was younger, I had owned horses and had ridden competitively. My relationship with horses, though, had become sickeningly jaded as a result of an abusive horseback-riding trainer who had turned my beloved equine companions into machines that were used until they broke down. After I returned from the treatment center, my parents encouraged me to begin horseback riding again. This time, though, I wouldn't be going back to my old trainer. Being around horses again was just what I needed at this dark time in my life. Horses gave me a sense of normalcy when nothing else was normal; a sense of purpose when nothing else seemed worth doing. More than anything, though, horses gave me a reason to wake up in the morning.

Yet, as before, I was still living for the sake of someone else. Before, it had been my parents. Now, it was horses. I was still not living because I was not honoring my life and myself.

It was not until I learned to value myself as a person that I began to truly heal and the sadness finally began to subside. The development of self-value was a slow and continues to be an ongoing process. It began once I entered therapy and realized for the first time that I am not my disorder. I am Melissa. This distinction between my disorders and me was like one of those great *ah ha* moments in my life. Before, I had viewed myself as a conglomeration of symptoms and a diagnostic axis full of disorders.

The recognition that I was a person, that I was valuable was the life-changing event that I still believe saved me from my depression. This awe-striking realization led me to nurture myself, both physically and emotionally. Instead of starving myself, I began to nourish my body with healthy meals. Instead, of blunting emotions, I began to allow myself to feel. That is not to say that things are all better now and that I never experience those old feelings of sadness. If I told you I was all better now, I would be lying to you. The difference now, though, is that I know I am valuable, because I am a person.

31

The Emotional Cost of Bankruptcy

By Michael D. Russo

I had always had an interest in building my own business. Not just any old corner store but a big enterprise. From the age of fourteen I had a desire to work for myself. My father set me up with some lawn mowing equipment and I knocked on doors after school and on the weekends to earn money. This was my first business. I continued to learn, read and discover as much about this capitalistic society as I could and I couldn't get enough of it.

Fast-forward a few years and I was married young, nineteen, and we had our first child a little over a year later. So now I still had all the desire in the world but with the responsibilities and family commitments of an older individual. I worked some more, learned some more, tried my hand at a lot of different things and finally after twelve years, I built my first million dollar business at the age of 26.

I began in real estate developing a multi-million dollar portfolio in only a few short years. I then expanded into retail developing a chain of stores. The plan was to develop our small chain into a national franchise and in the process of attempting this we grew too fast, ran out of working capital and ended up homeless and eventually bankrupt to the tune of $3.5 million. At the time I was supporting my wife and two young children and the experience changed us for life.

It would be nice to say that there were mitigating factors to my collapse, and there were, but the truth of the matter was I made most of the mistakes new entrepreneurs make and had to take full responsibility for my own actions.

None of which prepared me for the emotional cost of my failure.

During this period of time in our lives I ended up sued, assaulted, received death threats, accused of fraud, defamed, homeless (twice) and eventually bankrupt. For a year I suffered nightmares of murder and suicide and at times was physically unable to move for weeks on end. I remember one time my sister and brother in law had called by to see how I was and I remember crawling from under the bed (because I couldn't get onto the bed) to the front door to open up for them. My muscles were locked from the tension and stress and I couldn't find any way to relax them.

I know that during this time my youngest sister was married but despite being in attendance (and many years since looking at the photos of the happy day), I have no recollection of actually being there. No matter how hard I have tried I cannot remember more than a few fleeting images of the day. In contrast to my other siblings who were married several years before my bankruptcy, which I remember, quite clearly like any other special occasion.

One of the biggest challenges I had to deal with was coming to the realization that many of my family and friends (most of whom should have known better) suddenly became my enemies and in some cases led the charge against me. When I was doing well, everyone was happy to be associated with me but when I fell, I quickly found out just how many people I could count on. There weren't many.

My relationship with my wife and children (especially my wife) became strained and although I am happy to stay we are still married and came through it together we have been scarred for life. The arguments, confusion, lack of stability, walkouts and lack of direction for our children are still all too vivid in my memory.

One of my investors decided that losing money in business, constitutes fraud and I arrived home one day to find 8 armed members of the fraud investigation squad with a warrant for search and seizure for my business documents. I found myself on my own couch answering questions about drug connections, guns, ties to terrorist organizations, and links to child pornography rings. I'll never forget the 'baby face' cop who was questioning me and thinking just how far from base he really was (as was the investor who felt such action was a reflection of my true character).

Twelve months later (the same twelve months that I suffered severe nightmares) all investigations were dropped, my files returned and no charges were ever laid. However, to this day I cannot look at a cop in uniform without feelings of injustice, anger and now have very little respect for their authority. Once the worst of it was over then the re-building process had to begin.

I'm not referring to the 'empire', I'm referring to the self-confidence, the self-image, the ability to let go and move forward, the talking voice in the back of my head that to this day still chatters away every time I try to do something out of the box.

For the three years after the bankruptcy, I found every venture or project I involved myself in on behalf of someone else went very well, but I couldn't make anything work well for myself. All my own projects never made it off the ground. I even put together a national welcome campaign for Oprah Winfrey's visit to Australia in 2010 on behalf of a client and it worked beautifully getting mainstream media coverage and reaching an audience of over 1 million people. Yet I was unable to earn any substantial income in the years following the bankruptcy.

We lived on income below the national poverty line and were continually moved from house to house because I couldn't manage to pay the rent. I went from owning over a dozen properties worth millions to being unable to pay the rent.

This slowly got better and I managed with counseling, patience and time to drag myself out of depression (which I would define as a long period of time being unable to help one's self). I still had many days after this when I would get so depressed (short periods of deep loss) that I would simply shut down to those around me. I would be there in body but not spirit. Going through the motions I think they call it. Not a lot of fun.

One of the activities I found that helped a lot was writing. I just began to write about my experiences and my lessons learned. It was very therapeutic for me as I was able to look upon those experiences from the point of view of a third party. It helped me get through.

As an entrepreneur you often hear the phrase that 'failure is a part of success'. Unfortunately when you're in the middle of a major financial meltdown saying 'failure is a part of success' doesn't really help much. It's doesn't bring back the money or assets, it doesn't restore hope or confidence in one's self or others and it doesn't put food on the table. So even though I knew this statement was true, it just made me mad. In fact, I spent almost all of this time mad! I yelled and snapped at anyone and everyone and lost a lot of faith in people much of which has still yet to be restored.

One of the most common questions I get in radio interviews or by other entrepreneurs is how I managed to get through this time intact. My answer is always the same. I don't really know. Most days I got up hoping *this day* would be better than the last (usually it wasn't) and just wanted to make it to the end without killing myself or someone else.

I was focused on the future being better. If I could live long enough and jump high enough, all of the obstacles would give way, and I could show my wife, children, friends, family and myself that what I was trying to achieve was possible.

Many times I also felt the divine hand of God guiding and protecting me. I guess I still had work to do.

I've heard of some people going through similar events and bouncing right back. Getting back on the horse, I think they call it. My experience was not like that. Despite my desire to still fight, I now realize that the 'loss' and subsequent 'grieving' period as I refer to it was necessary. It was part of the healing process.

Depression is real but it also manifests itself in different ways for different people. Some have a much better handle of life's challenges than others. Finding a way to cope is also an individual thing.

Counseling, prayer and support from a handful of loved ones got me through. It would be a lie to say it didn't change my outlook on life though. I'm far less likely to jump into the middle of things like I used to. I lost much of my spontaneity and self-confidence and I'm not sure that's always for the better.

Our experiences are supposed to make use grow; mine have made me that much more cautious. Still, it's all part of life's adventure. I'm really looking forward to surpassing my former status soon and sharing that joy with my family who supported me through this period of my life. I know one thing for sure, without my wife and children, I wouldn't be here today.

32

In Search of Sleep

By Leigh Kramer

My battle with sleep goes way back to childhood. I always resisted going to bed. I begged for one more story, one more glass of water, one more anything just to stay up a little later. One such story involved my parents putting me to bed, only to deal with my request for a hug, which I'm sure melted their irritated hearts. I then complained there was something in my eye. When they addressed each issue and sent me back to my room, I cried, "There's something in my knee!" Needless to say, I still had to go to bed that night and each thereafter.

I am a night owl. I enjoy a good night's sleep as much as anyone. I just don't want to miss out on anything. I was the queen of every sleepover and youth group lock-in. Around junior high, my night-loving ways changed into insomnia. This was also when depression entered my life. I couldn't shut my mind off and the lack of sleep left me unable to filter out my self-hate.

"You're ugly. No one loves you. No one will miss you. You're so dumb." Tapes played repeatedly about my perceived failures, even at age 13. After hours lying there, quietly sobbing so as not to disturb my family, I would eventually drift to sleep. Even once the depression lifted, my sleep struggles remained, stuck in this horrible habit.

I've never been able to fall asleep right away, no matter how tired I might be. Thirty minutes before sleep takes hold is a good night in my book. Insomnia returned in times of stress throughout high school, college, and grad school. For the most part it was manageable. Or I was overly used to thriving on little sleep. I figured that sleep problems would just be a part of my life, my personal scar from surviving depression.

Then I reached my breaking point. I was managing only a few hours of sleep a night. There was no end in sight. Though I'd unsuccessfully tried various remedies before, it was time to seek help. I'd been lax on seeing a doctor the past few years. Since I was a healthy 27 year old, I never found a replacement doctor when mine went on a retainer service. My mom encouraged me to see her doctor, Dr. Sullivan.

It didn't go as planned. I arrived at the medical building ready to figure out the root of my insomnia. I arrived in his office primed to cry in front of a stranger. The signs were there: heart hammering, throat tightening, and eyes welling. I did not want to cry there.

I knew why I was close to crying. Grandma had died two weeks prior. I worked, at the time, as a hospice social worker. There was no way to escape death, loss, or bereavement issues. Grief sucks. To top it off, I'd seen Mom in the waiting room before meeting with Dr. Sullivan. She'd just seen him and confided that she'd shared about her mother's death. As with all of our recent conversations, we became teary in those few minutes before I was called back.

I purposely blanked my mind, willing the tears to go away. I wanted to appear competent on my first visit with this doctor. It worked for a while.

Dr. Sullivan set me at ease with his smile and the way he actually looked at me. How many doctors maintain eye contact? It was a good sign. I mentioned I wanted to deal with my insomnia. He didn't appear overly concerned. Bad sign. However, he listened, which put him back in the Good Sign category. We went on to review my health history, with the double whammy of cancer on my mom's side of the family and cardiac issues on my dad's side of the family.

When we came to the mental health history of the exam, I took a deep breath and shared. I didn't sugarcoat my past depression. I talked easily about what I've been through because it is firmly in the past. I was depressed and at one time suicidal. I hadn't been depressed in well over a decade.

Based on my journals and recollections of that time, I believe I was clinically depressed in junior high. I never told anyone my feelings at the time and therefore did not receive an official diagnosis or treatment. After becoming a Christian in 8th grade, I no longer wanted to kill myself but I never learned how to repair my self-esteem and correct negative thinking. In fact, I wouldn't go on to see a counselor until after my freshman year of college when I became tired of the inevitable downward spiral.

Going to counseling was one of my best decisions. Who I was then is light years from who I am now. Dr. Sullivan didn't know any of this, however. There's no way to share 14 years of struggle and victory in a 20-minute exam.

A teachable moment in which I remembered why it's important to have regular doctor visits. When something changes or there's a problem, the doctor already knows you and your history and can differentiate between the symptoms and causes. Dr. Sullivan had no such advantage.

He had me, my health history, and the choice to believe me or not.

He was a good doctor but I saw the light in his eyes as he grappled with my depression history. He didn't believe that people could break free from depression. I gave him credit though. He asked me about recent stressors.

The visit went downhill before I saw we were at its edge. All the blithe sharing about past pain was pushed to the side as present day pain took center stage. I had to talk about Grandma. The Leigh of Junior High was not the Leigh that finds herself a grandmother short. I could not sit in front of this man and talk about my grandmother without remembering her smile, her amazing coffee cake, her hospitality, and her faith. I could not talk about her without realizing anew that I would never see her again, that she will not watch me walk down the aisle one day or take a 4 generation portrait as I hold my future daughter.

While my heart hammered and throat tightened, I couldn't stop the tears from coming. My professional tear-stopping tricks failed. I was mortified, face flushed and still the tears fell. I *knew* how it looked.

I handed him the ammunition he needed to make his diagnosis.

History of Depression + Crying + Insomnia = Current Depression

He handed me my first prescription for an anti-depressant.

"But I'm not depressed." I told him. "I'm grieving. There's a difference."

I wasn't in denial and I wasn't depressed. I tried explaining it to him. Depression is different from grief. They both have yawning chasms, to be sure. However, I rested in hope. One day I would see my grandmother again in heaven. When I was depressed, I could not see outside of myself enough to see that the world did not end in junior high. As much pain as I felt now, I knew it wouldn't last to the same degree forever.

He smiled and nodded, in a way that would feel patronizing if I weren't so exhausted. He told me that the medication would help with my insomnia and level everything else out.

I needed to sleep. I was desperate for an answer. I pretended that Dr. Sullivan prescribed the medication because it really would help me.

The medication did not help. Nauseated, I barely ate the first two weeks. No one ever minds unintentional weight loss but I did miss eating. This would have been bearable if my sleep had in fact improved. The medication made my insomnia worse. It took me even longer to fall asleep and I woke up more often during the night. Now, thanks to this medication, I was exhausted and starving.

I tapered off the anti-depressant. Once it was out of my system, I went back to my familiar brand of insomnia. I then headed to the library and checked out 10 books on sleep disorders. I was determined to find an answer. Enough was enough. It was time my body learned another way to respond to stress and grief.

I decided to try a sleep schedule. Waking up and going to bed at the same time every day, only staying in bed for the amount of sleep you need. I figured seven and a half hours was my ideal, so I went to bed at 11:30 pm and woke up at 7 am. Even on the weekends. If I stayed up later than 11:30 pm, I still had to get up at 7 am.

It was brutal at first. But it worked.

It's been almost 4 years since I saw Dr. Sullivan. Insomnia is now a rare occurrence. If I ever have a sleepless night, I examine my stress level and figure out how to adjust my self-care routine. I'm more in tune with myself. I handle the every day ups and downs of life more easily because I am more rested.

I went to the doctor in search of sleep. I came out affirming my growth and my survival. My past depression may mark me but it will never define me.

33

Coming Out of the Dark

By Jenny Susa

Depression is becoming increasingly common and statistics show that one person commits suicide in America every 15 minutes. When I was a teenager, I could have been one of those statistics. And since adulthood, two people who had been my dear friends growing up became a part of those numbers, as well as an acquaintance, a good friend's father, another friend's uncle, and several people whose names I had never heard until people started talking about the untimely death they chose for themselves. I had spoken out about overcoming depression when I was a lot younger but the older I grew, I got away from sharing my story because it seemed as if it had happened a whole lifetime ago and there was no reason to discuss it anymore.

When my last friend ended his own life last year, I felt God calling me to tell as many people as possible that there is always a better way.

I remembered how it felt to want to end my own life because I couldn't see a way out of my daily emotional pain. I went to this friend's funeral and heard people questioning how he could do this to his family. I recalled being so lost in hopelessness and self-loathing that I thought my own family would be better off without me. I remembered how God had brought me through that time of darkness, and I realized that I had not kept passing along the important truth that depression can be overcome.

I was brought up in a Christian home with two parents who loved each other and their kids. But our household was not without its share of turmoil. I had one older brother who I used to think was very cool, but he didn't want any part of hanging out with me. The two of us are as different as night and day, so we constantly clashed and he said a lot of hurtful things to me. The problem was that being a young girl with such low self-esteem, I took all of his comments to heart and believed them. In addition to the negativity between us, there was my dad, who just like me, has a hot temper. At that time in his life, he rarely showed emotions other than anger, and had the tendency towards saying a lot of things he probably didn't mean. I couldn't understand this at my young age, and again his negative words resonated in my mind over and over, and I felt unloved by everyone in my family except my mom.

Trying to fit in at school was just as difficult for me. It was my first year of junior high and I had troubles with all of the older girls, who eventually started up some rumors about me. Everyone who has been to high school knows that rumors don't have to be true for people to believe them. I went to school every day feeling ugly, stupid, and worthless. I went home to what I perceived was a family who didn't want me around. I went to bed early at night because I felt like it was the only time the world would just leave me alone. I dreamed of ways to end my pointless life. My mom, who was the only person I believed cared at all, was my first saving grace. I said things to her about how I thought everyone would be better off if I wasn't there, and she asked me, "What do you think I would do without you?" I didn't want to hurt my mom so I held back from doing anything to follow through on my thoughts.

My parents started taking me to a Christian counselor, and it didn't take long for this special person to help me see the truth. I believe the devil is always working to make people believe things that aren't true, and at this young age, when everything was so unbalanced for me, I believed a lot of lies. I thought I was a worthless individual whom no one cared about, and that I had nothing special to offer.

My counselor reminded me that I was a creation of God, and that God doesn't make mistakes. He created me for a purpose, and the same is true of every person in the world. God places all of us here to accomplish different things for Him, but part of everyone's purpose is just to have a relationship with our Creator. He loved us before he made us, only wanting us to love Him in return.

I believed in God since I was a child and would have always said that I loved Him, but I didn't understand his complete perfection, and how he brings everyone to the world prepared to direct our paths, and give us peace through all circumstances, if we will allow Him to do that.

From my experience, it is a life long growth process in one's relationship with God that shows us how to depend on Him for peace. If we understand His word and that His promises apply to all of us who love Him, God can make something good out of anything. "Cast all your anxiety on him because he cares for you." (1 Peter 5:7 NIV) All I need to do for peace of mind is remember that the Creator of the universe cares for every one of us enough to give the life of His son. We are told to give our burdens to Him because He can handle them for us, better than we can by trying to rely on our own strength.

Because I received help from someone who knew how to give it, I came to an important realization that I have been able to hold onto throughout my entire life. Who was I to tell the Creator of the universe that I, his creation, had no value? I became a born again Christian later that year and the truth finally settled into my heart and mind. I was not ugly, stupid, or unworthy of love, but someone who Jesus would say had great value. So much so that even the hairs of my head are numbered. I was someone who God blessed with certain gifts, so that I could be a blessing to others, just like he has done for everyone. I was someone He made for a reason, someone who God had plans for, someone who was actually capable of doing all things through Christ.

Within my sadness of losing friends and seeing the wonderful things they will miss because they felt their lives were not worth living, I looked back at all the joys of my lifetime and couldn't believe I would have missed it all if I had not accepted the help available to me, and instead followed through on what I originally wanted to do. Of all those amazing things, the blessing that never would have existed would have been my son, Lucas. It happens that he is facing special circumstances in his own life because of Fragile X Syndrome, but that is another story all by itself. I will just say that even though he is only four years old, we can already see that he is going to help change the world in his own way. If I had chosen to leave this world before my time, my beautiful, precious child would not be here.

My life has not been without trouble. Jesus said in John 16:33:

> *"In this world you will have trouble, but take heart, I have overcome the world."*

I still face seasonal depression year after year, and even though I know it is coming and try to be preemptive, that devil will always use the gray days of winter to work on me. I have had hard days where all I want to do is cry because I think that whatever challenges we are facing seem completely impossible.

The difference in me over the last several years and the girl I was at 13, is that I understand that troubles pass, and no matter what storms you might face throughout the course of your life, the Lord promises that you don't have to face it alone. He can erase your self-doubt the way he did for me. He can give you strength for the day and peace in the midst of your problems. Because I hold onto His word, pray a lot and turn to friends who I know will do the same, I have been able to tackle my seasonal depression without medication.

Depression is the most treatable form of mental illness there is, and nobody should ever be ashamed to seek help. People may have to overcome depression in different ways, but the first step is always to talk to someone who can help you. I also encourage everyone to find out more about Jesus if you don't know him, because his gift of salvation and the promises of God's word are what have brought me through every dark hour of my life. With God on my side, nothing of this world has ever been able to keep me down. I will end with my favorite promise from God, because I understand that everyone we meet in life might be facing something very difficult and wondering why they have to if there is a God who loves them. The promise that always brings me through the challenges of life is this...

> Romans 8:28 - And we know that in all things God works for the good of those who love him, who have been called according to his purpose.

34

Hope Heals

By Melody Harrison Hanson

"I will search for my lost ones who strayed away and I will bring them safely home again. I will bandage the injured and strengthen the weak..." (Ezekiel 34:16 - NLT)

This is the story of how I fell into the sinkhole of depression and climbed my way out again. My story began with pride and self-delusion and moved to healing and acceptance—forgiving myself for being less than I imagined. The path of brokenness took me to frightening, even diabolical places, but God found me in the pit of my depression, tenderly loving me as I accepted my raging need for him. Finally, in my forties, after a decade of turmoil, the crooked path led to hope and healing. Writing this, going back and lingering, has been harder than I expected. I offer it here because of what God has done in me.

When I quit my job to be a stay-at-home mom, I was unprepared for how unhappy I became. Forever seeing my life in terms of success or failure, I believed that I was failing. What kind of a mother doesn't love being at home with her children? Over the years we shared long, sunburnt summer days at the pool and sweaty bike rides but, even as we meandered through the zoo and the farmer's market, I grew increasingly restless and miserable. If I was truthful, I had been frantic and dissatisfied at work. Leaving was more like running away under the ruse of caring for the kids. For years my job had buoyed me up on the raging ocean of my insecurities and fear of failure. Going home took away that life preserver. I had never dealt with the need every human being has for purpose and significance. I had nowhere left to run!

I was at that time incapable of being happy at work or at home, battling the haunting, negative tape loops in my head repeating vicious lies. They drove me, making my life joyless and full of fear. My misery eroded my self-esteem, telling me that I would never find the community I longed for; that I was a terrible mother, employee, boss, friend, lover, sister, and artist; and that I had no reason for hope. From childhood these lies defined me. As my core identity, they pushed me. Fear of failure motivated me to work harder than others, inevitably becoming a workaholic. Being at home became a nightmare that I was too proud to admit I was living. The voices taunted me, whispering, "Surely, *anyone* can be a mother, why can't you just do it and be happy about it?" I was failing at the "easy" job of motherhood by being unhappy. I had a lot to learn. In my most fearful moments I still have intense regret for walking away from my career. It is only in retrospect that I clearly see the loving hand of God. He eventually used the negative voices to heal and restore me by speaking back to them. I have come to believe that God pulled me from of the grind of the workplace out of love.

When depression hit it was an excruciating slide over many months—slowly, hypnotically gripping and weakening my body, soul, and me. The irrational thoughts would sit with me for days, taunting me, berating me, and making my waking hours a living hell. Without a full understanding of what was happening to me, I thought I was going mad. Too anxious to sleep well at night, I became confused and overwhelmed by small decisions. Alcohol dulled the anxiety and ache in my belly, but it gradually grew into dependency. I later learned that alcohol is a depressant, the worst choice for someone who struggles with depression, and that chemical dependency runs in families, including my own.

In the spring of 2002, with three small children climbing over and around me I felt myself slip into a prison of my own making. With no one to counter them, the lies were now vilifying me relentlessly. For me, the crooked road to sanity came by risking the humiliation of telling someone. It is a vulnerable thing to tell someone that you are dejected and unhappy, perhaps even depressed. Uttering those words was crucial—a key to opening my heart to God's brilliant rays of truth about myself. It was after five weeks of suffering alone through the longest days imaginable that I blurted out to my husband one day, "I think I may be depressed." We didn't know anything about the illness at the time and we had no idea how bad things would get before they got better. Admitting it was the beginning of healing for me.

For the first time in my life I looked squarely at myself—discovering that I had no idea *who* I was. I did not feel lovable. I desperately wanted to be doing something *"significant"* with my talent. I felt that what I was doing was not significant *enough*. And though I had always professed to be a Christ-follower, I did not *feel* the love and acceptance of being Yahweh's beloved, precious child. *With my pretenses gone, left only with the charade, I shattered into a million pieces.*

I spent months doing the hard work of therapy. That winter, with depression still a daily affliction and life continuing to be inconceivably hard, we learned that the odd symptoms my father was experiencing were the result of brain cancer. He was given a few months. Convinced that I couldn't cope, I sought medication from my psychiatrist. In order to take an antidepressant, I had to confirm that I was not pregnant because there is no research on the impact of antidepressants on a fetus. I was getting on the plane to my parents when I got the call that I was, indeed, pregnant. Time stood still as I absorbed the idea of an unplanned pregnancy at the moment that I needed lifesaving medication. It was a decision that my husband and I anguished over and had finally made.

The next four days at my parents, I ignored my problems. My sisters and I found ourselves helping our dad, who was exhibiting mania induced by the pressure on his skull, while we watched our mother fall apart. She had been his full-time caregiver and because we were there, she let go—going on a 24 hour crying jag and drinking heavily.

That weekend I had a panic attack in a grocery store where I was picking up a medication for my mom. As the pharmacist reminded me that my mother should not drink alcohol with the medication, I came apart. It felt like a heart attack. I sank to the floor, clutching myself, paralyzed with anxiety. Though I desperately wanted to, I could not ignore the issues I brought with me. At some point I slowly came back to myself, got up from the floor where I crumbled, and drove to my parents. I shut the door to the small basement room that I occupied.

Again I found myself on the floor, this time prostrate on my knees, utterly humbled, crying out to God. Despair flowed out of me as I gave it all over. I laid it at Jesus' feet. I gave him my fears—that

I might always be depressed; that I might never be able to forgive my parents; and that I might always have a propensity to question everything, especially spiritual things. God met me there in the pain and panic and total devastation of my heart, the scared, private place that no one sees. And that day God promised me that if I lived for him, no matter what the future held, he would walk it with me. Out of that knowledge God has given me the courage to forgive myself. I received grace, peace and hope. And this began a transformation that continues to this day.

The Word of God heals me. It speaks regularly to the false voices that want to dominate my mind. It became a new foundation to rebuild myself on and my lifeline. For the first time in my life, I was able to give and receive love. And I do not need my fear and self-loathing to motivate me to excellence.

My husband fought hard for me, always believing that it was possible to heal. We lost the baby early in the pregnancy through miscarriage and this was devastating, as I deeply desired a fourth child. I dream of her and know that I will be with her in glory, as well as my father who died within a few months. Many times it was my husband's hope that I depended on, even as God kept his promise and walked with me every step of the way. Eventually I admitted my own alcoholism and have been sober nearly three years now. Working on my pathological need to be perfect, I made a conscious effort to be gentle with myself and built space into life for healing, which sometimes feels slow, but God's timing is perfect. I have faced the lifelong loneliness of childhood and risked seeking out meaningful community. And today, I have found equilibrium with fewer depressive episodes each year. The grace and hope of God continues to heal me.

I have been running from sorrow my entire life. Depression

and recovery forced me to stop. God found me in the pit of my desperation, misery and shame.

There is gentleness to accepting rather than resisting God and his timing. If I look at my episodes of depression as Ecclesiastical seasons, I have lived through seasons of isolation and loss and seasons of drowning in an ocean of tears, afraid of life and mourning my secrets. I now find hope in the promised seasons of laughter and joy, of healing and hope, of planting and growing, of holding on tight to those I love.

Even though I have been learning and healing, there are still times when I am completely undone by doubt, restlessness and an inner turmoil. A strange melancholy comes over me—an unsettling of my soul, an irritation, and distrust. I have a heightened awareness of my voluminous, endless need, which is a way for God to capture my attention, yet again. If I open myself to him, he meets me.

Ecclesiastes says it well:

> *"But in the end, does it really make a difference what anyone does? I've had a good look at what God has given us to do—busywork, mostly. True, God made everything beautiful in itself and in its time—but he's left us in the dark, so we can never know what God is up to, whether he's coming or going. ...Whatever God does, that's the way it's going to be, always. No addition, no subtraction. God's done it and that's it. That's so we'll quit asking questions and simply worship in holy fear. Whatever was, is. Whatever*

will be, is. That's how it always is with God."

(Ecclesiastes 3:9–15, MSG)

I now believe that it does not matter to God what I "do" with my life. He simply wants my worship and my whole heart. When the pain of this life was too much for me, and I could no longer bury my sorrow, I traveled a crooked path into the sinkhole of depression. I was rescued and what I found through that was the mystery of God's perfect love. We do not journey into depression alone—I know this now, fully. Though I wandered and felt alone as I fell deeply into depression, God searched for me and he found me. My hope and peace are in the fact that God remains with me now and always.

This promise is true for everyone. God will find you in the pit of your depression and pain. And all that he asks of you in that moment is to give him your heart. That is the hope that heals.

35

My Darkest Hour

By Allison Carroll

Depression is a horrible mistress. I have long suffered with her ever since I can remember. Even as a child I knew she was there, I just never knew what to call her. When you exist in a state of depression you have a very vague sense of true reality. The only reality you know is the one you exist in at the moment.

Reflecting back on those times of darkness, I am never able to grasp the full scope of them. I often write during my times of depression. It helps me to try to put things into perspective. After one of my most recent bouts of severe depression, I discovered some things I had written during that time. The following are some of those writings.

> *"Lost doesn't even begin to describe how it feels to be in the pit I keep finding myself at the bottom of. How the hell do I keep winding up here? I am so dysfunctional! What is my problem? Where does this darkness come from? It has occurred to me that I may not have fallen into a pit at all. I may actually exist in this pit all of*

the time.

Sometimes I am surrounded by light and I can see clearly for 360 degrees all around me. But sometimes there is no light, only darkness. That is when I realize where I really am. My delusions of grandeur are laid to rest and I am able to see that the reality of my life is that I live in isolation. I am isolated from everyone and out of the sight of God. I realize that I have no one but myself and my own heart. I don't like that because my heart is rancid. When the pit grows dark and the world grows silent I can hear the beating of that ugly heart. It beats louder and louder, screaming out its ugliness until I can't take it anymore and I want it to die. I want it to stop. I want my heart to stop beating. I want my wretched heart to stop hurting and for my mind to stop thinking. It is horrible. But I want to die.

It's not scary here in my darkness. It is dreadful listening to the sound of my ugly, beating heart but I am not afraid. There is a sort of melancholy that exists in this world. It is very simple and matter of fact. My thoughts are not simple; they are convoluted and complicated to be sure. But there is no fear. Drifting away into nothingness would be a relief for me. The only concern I have is for those who will be left behind me and what it will do to them. That is how I live my life. I am always serving other people and their feelings. I am always worried about someone being indisposed or unsettled on my account.

Sometimes I think about what everyone's life would be like if I didn't exist. I am so tired. I am exhausted mentally, spiritually and physically. I don't know how much longer I can go on. My body is tired and my mind and heart are hurting. I have been told, and have mostly believed that God has forgiven me for committing adultery. He has responded to my cries for mercy and has taken my sin and thrown it as far as the east is from the west. But forgiving myself is a totally different thing. It is sinful according to the Bible for me to be unforgiving towards myself.

I have learned to suck it up and move on because I have responsibilities and there are some things I just can't walk away from. Sucking it up really sucks in itself. Who wants to do that all the time? Not me. No one does. Some never do and some never have to. That's not fair. But what is?"

Reading those words on this side of my depression is very hard to do. It gives me a look into the dark abyss in which I existed but from a much different perspective. The depression was turning me into someone who was nothing like the person that I really am. Now I am at the top of the pit looking down at myself and I can see that even though all I could see in the midst of my depression was hopelessness, there was a light at the end of the tunnel and it wasn't a train. It was my life patiently waiting for me to come back to reality.

I would say that no one likes to wake up to discover writing like that. It's crude, rough and sickening. I stood silent and tried to process it all while the questions whirred around from my heart to my brain to my gut while all the while I was forced to keep my composure. I had to keep it together and remain calm and composed on the outside while my insides endured the storm. The silence that was required for that was deafening. It was damaging not only to my heart, mind and body, but to my spirit. It welled up and collected inside of my soul like vomit at the back of my throat but I had to choke it down. I couldn't let anyone see the vile, disgusting substance that I was holding back. I told myself over and over, "Keep it together, keep it together, breathe, breathe." It is very difficult to understand the life that others are living until you live it yourself.

From the outside, things look like they are tied into a neat and tidy package. They are enticing and worthy of envy. Once you enter the reality of it yourself you start to see things in a different light. Slowly things are revealed. The good, the bad, and the ugly. It is all there in your face. Sometimes it slaps you with a harsh reality. The shock of that reality lasts a long time. It takes time for things to become clear.

Piece by piece you are handed clues and doses of reality until eventually they start to form a picture. Along the way you may think you know what the picture is going to look like but little by little it changes until eventually it all starts to come together. And what you are looking at is not what you thought it was going to be at all. You may love the new revelation and stand in awe of its grand magnificence. Or you may stand there with your head spinning and your mouth agape struggling to make sense of your once warped sense of reality.

I believe that I will be able to use these writings from my depressive state as a navigation tool if I am ever lost again. They will be a sign of hope to me that when I am in my darkest hour, there will someday be sunshine again. I have shared these writings with my husband, Ray in the hopes that if I ever find myself at the bottom of that pit again they will also help him to remind me that he and my life will be waiting for me to return.

36

Bridges

By Jason N. Wright

I have always liked to take long walks. Or rather I tend to take long walks. Sometimes for the exercise, sometimes for the view and sometimes just to think. Since rivers divide my town, it is hard to get far without crossing a bridge. For most people, bridges are a convenient way to get from here to there. I suspect that few people give much thought to design and building materials used to construct them. Fewer still know the history of a given bridge--when it was constructed, whether any battles were fought over it during a war, or the distance one would have to travel to reach the same destination if a particular bridge were not present.

For much of my life, I was a bit of a connoisseur of area bridges, but my fascination was far more morbid. From puberty until at least my early 30's, I studied and speculated as to the consequences of jumping from each of them, should the "need" arise. The railroad trestle near my parents' home was usually not more than about 30 feet from the deck to the river at its highest point, and was almost certainly a safe jump. In fact, each summer we kids, who lived near it, did just that on a fairly routine basis. After all, the meter platform is a regular event for some Olympic divers. It is barely dangerous and far from lethal. On the other hand, the trestle is out of the way, far from foot and auto traffic, making interruption unlikely.

If I were sufficiently determined, I might weigh myself down somehow, with cement blocks perhaps. But that is just so…complicated. Of course, there were the seasons to consider. Conditions that may have otherwise been less than favorable to suicide can change with the seasons, and a jump into the same river in January could have a very different result from one in July. And what of the other bridges? They are highly trafficked, so there will probably be witnesses and a rescue attempt. Hell, the county rescue squad station flanks one. This is not a good thing if one does not want to be rescued. Besides, is 50 or 60 feet enough to be lethal? Though I would not try it for myself just for fun, I have seen people jump from greater heights with no negative effects. There are things to jump from, of course, but for whatever reason, a bridge was always my plan of choice. Fewer cleanups for those left behind, I suppose.

I did not always have these thoughts when crossing bridges, nor did I always set out on a walk with the intention of thinking about anything different than anyone else on the road. But I must admit, I have set out on walks from which my return was less than assured. It has now been a few years since I last took one of *those* walks and I am reasonably confident that it was the *last* one I will ever take. In retrospect, the catalyst for the walk certainly did not warrant such drastic action, but does anything, really? It wasn't the first stupid and insignificant cause for this kind of walk. Once, a girl I liked, but never dated, seemed to go out of her way to ignore me. Another girl dumped me. My car broke down and I didn't think I could afford the repair, so I almost jumped on my way to a telephone to get help. No bill to worry about. My company transferred me from one store to another against my wishes.

This time it wasn't a girl or a bill. This time it felt more personal, more real and more burdensome. Someone I respected thought I didn't sing well and took steps to prevent me from singing in church. He was probably right. I *don't* sing well. At least not as well as the people on the radio or concert stage. I'm "pitchy," I don't pronounce vowels correctly and my voice is just kind of harsh sounding. But I had been a part of the church band for a while and at the time, such harsh criticism felt like the end of my world. I wanted to die. Or at least hurt myself in a very significant way. I could jump. I could cut myself with kitchen knives. I could try jumping headlong through the picture window at home. The desire to do something, *anything,* that would show the world outside what I was feeling like inside was overwhelming.

That is what sucks about depression. To the uninitiated, depression is just foreign. It is like being a civilian hanging around the V.F.W. They understand the words and the stories, but they have no idea what it is really like to experience it firsthand. Depression is not rational. Depression does not care. Depression mocks its victims with its lack of any hard physical evidence. There is no blood test with results to show that there is a "real" disease at work. This disease plagued me for much of my life. Every year, I missed weeks to months of school for "fatigue." Every Christmas, I wondered how people could be having such a good time when all I wanted to do was stay in bed. Some mornings, I was genuinely disappointed to have awoken. For the longest time, I don't think I even grasped that other people didn't feel this way. I just figured they were better at faking their way through it than I was.

When I was told I (literally) couldn't sing my long-time fascination with bridges started to come to a head. I had studied them before, but that night, I really wanted a close look. I tried to get to the catwalk under one of the bridges to avoid scrutiny and unwanted attention. I had been on it before, but now a gate had been installed that served as a significant impediment to reaching it. I climbed up to street level and looked down. It didn't feel right. I went to another bridge and looked down from at least four different spots, some over land and some over water. I could "see" myself just letting go. Were I not married, if I had no kids or friends, that may well have been it. But the only thing worse than the pain I was feeling myself was the pain I knew I would cause them if I went through with it. I was hurting. I wanted others to hurt. But not my family. There was no way to hurt myself without hurting others.

I was reaching a crossroads. Clearly the guy that felt like this so much of the time was not going to make it to his forties. By this time, I was finally diagnosed as being bipolar and had begun receiving some proper care and medication, but such things were only going to be as effective as I let them. So I gave in, not to the disease but to the love of those around me. My worth would not be bound up in talent or material success or membership in this faith community or that clique. I began to figure out that mental illness might be something that I have, but it is not what I am. Disease is not a moral failing.

That is not to say that I simply flipped a switch. I have not been cured. It is unlikely that I ever will be. But I let the doctors and medications do their job, and I began to hold up my end of the bargain. I am better about speaking up. I am better at living and not merely being alive. I took control. I underwent therapy. I went back to college and finished my degree. I joined groups that share my interests. In short, after more than two decades of alternately ignoring pain or giving into it, I found a way not to hurt, as least not as much.

As for the bridges? Well, I am still fascinated by them, but now, when I look down, it is to better see the shimmering sunlight on the river's surface, or to imagine what it would be like to own a Jet ski. The idea that I would want to jump just seems foreign, as if it was somebody else thinking those thoughts. I like to think it was.

37

You Are Not Alone

By Tamara Lunardo

I write about everything, all the time. It's how I live, even when it's not how I make a living-- it is what makes me feel most alive. Writing is necessary for me; it comes out like an exhaled breath. And, perhaps emboldened by its ease, I'm not afraid to venture into the uncomfortable, to push perceived boundaries, to ask hard questions and leave them hanging in preference over a too-easy answer. I can write about almost anything.

But I can scarcely write this.

I've only just begun it, but I can already tell you: Writing about depression is hard. Writing about my faltering faith, my personality defects, my physical flaws, my parenting struggles-- that's easy. That's stuff everyone goes through; I know I'm not alone. But Depression is a sinister demon, and it's a damn good liar, and it loves to whisper, "You're all alone."

Writing about depression when I'm not having an episode is hard because it forces reflection on something so dark. But writing about it in the midst of it would be impossible. When Depression attacks, sometimes the most I can do is just get out of bed, and even that is unwelcome and trying. Forget productivity. Fuck creativity.

Depression strips me of my energy until I am barely useless. I sleep, and I sleep, and I sleep, and still I am tired. Body-tired, mind-tired, soul-tired—dead tired. I can have a full night's sleep and still resent the morning alarm: I am not nearly ready to do life. Every interaction, every small errand, every daily task is a laborious chore. I take a long nap not out of luxury but out of necessity, and even so, I cannot awake refreshed. The brief sleep has only been an escape; it has been respite, not rest.

Depression overcomes me with its brute power and I am helpless to fight it off; exhausted, my mind and my heart succumb. The voice of truth is dampened to a distant murmur when I can make it out at all, and I hear instead the insidious insistence of Depression's lies. It tells me that there is no one who sees or hears my pain, and even if there were, there is certainly no one who cares enough to touch it. And I listen, and I believe.

My husband, normally my strongest ally, appears to me condemning and uncaring. He asks me to take a walk in the sunshine because he knows it is healing; I hear him calling me crazy. He takes the children out because he knows I need quiet; I see him leaving me alone.

Depression toys with my emotions so that I am alternately weepy and apathetic. Both everything and nothing at all can make me cry-- sobs that go soul-deep and find no catharsis and begin again. Nothing brings comfort, nothing can be made right because no "thing" is the cause. Everything feels wrong. All feels hopeless. I can only cry out despair.

And then, mood changed out of nowhere explicable, I will be

unmovable. My normally soft heart will not care, cannot care, about anything or anyone. Not my closest friends. Not my loving husband. Not my precious children. And this last is the worst-- too awful to admit. What mother can see the beautiful, innocent faces of her own children and wholly look away? I loathe the monster apathy makes of me, and Depression gets off at its own sick game.

But although it lies, Depression is half right when it says that no one understands, because some of the people closest to me do not have to fight this particular demon, so they cannot grasp its power. They think I ought to snap out of it, shrug it off, perk up, rejoin life, and carry on as usual. But what they don't understand is that I am not free to do any of those things. I am captive. I am bound.

The walks in sunshine, the quiet, the offered walnuts and teas and assorted home remedies, they can lift and refresh me when the depression is just a small dip. But when that demon Depression is attacking full-force, it laughs in the face of impotent opponents, and I am not let go until it is damn well done with me.

Others, out of well-intentioned, utterly useless ignorance, may point to my Christian faith and say, "You're too blessed to be depressed." And their trite rhymes poke new pain in a deep wound. I am keenly aware of my tremendous blessings; that even they are not enough to wrest me from Depression's beastly grip is reason all the more for despair. If God has set His love on me, if Jesus has borne all my burdens, if I am truly made a new creation by the indwelt Spirit, then how, how am I so held captive still? As many times as I have been attacked by this demon, I have turned to my Savior and begged, "Why?" I don't know that I'll find an answer in this life.

But I do know a few things. Writing about depression is hard-- but I have done it here. Reading about depression is hard-- but you have done it now. Living through it alone is harder--but we need do it no more. And this is the one thing I know as surely as I write to live: There's nothing like writing down a book full of truth to stick it to a liar.

You are not alone.

About The Authors

Foreword: Elizabeth Esther is a mother of five and a popular blogger at www.elizabethesther.com.

Preface: Jonathan Brink is Senior Editor and Publisher at Civitas Press. He is learning daily what is means to live into the footsteps of Jesus. He is the author of *Discovering the God Imagination, Reconstructing A Whole New Christianity* (Civitas, 2010). He blogs regularly at jonathanbrink.com.

Introductions: Alise Wright is married to her best friend Jason and is the mom to four incredible kids. She loves writing, knitting, playing keyboards in a cover band, and eating soup. She writes about faith, family and friendship regularly at her blog, alise-write.com.

Awareness

Chapter 1: Matt Cannon is a husband, father, pastor, writer, and nerd. His writings have been featured in *The Knoxville News-Sentinel, The Baptist* and *Reflector*, and other local publications. He writes regularly on his blog at http://seekingpastor.wordpress.com. Matt lives in Knoxville, TN with his wife and five kids. He seeks to live, laugh, and love like Jesus and help others do the same. You can follow him on Twitter by searching for @seekingpastor.

Chapter 2: Laura Droege is an aspiring author who is querying agents about her first novel, *The Cruelest Month*. The novel was inspired by her experiences with bipolar depression during her pregnancies. Currently, she is writing a second novel, blogging, and learning the ins-and-outs of social media. Laura lives in Huntsville, Alabama, with her husband and two children. She loves to read, bake and exercise.

Chapter 3: Anonymous is a grateful daughter of the Lord God Almighty, saved by His grace through Jesus Christ.

Chapter 4: David Henson is a writer who lives in Georgia. He received his Master of Arts from the Graduate Theological Union in Berkeley, California. His meditations on scripture have appeared in the Episcopal Church's *Ready the Way: A Walk through Advent* (2009), *Patheos*, and the *Christian Century* Web site. He authors the blog *unorthodoxology*. A former journalist, his work has appeared in *The Oakland Tribune, Seattle Post-Intelligencer, Coastal Living* magazine and various other publications.

Chapter 5: Laura E. Crook was born and raised outside of Boston, went to college in Chicago and currently lives in Los Angeles. She has a Bachelors in Television Writing and in her spare time she writes teen dramas for television and drinks too much Coca-Cola. When she grows up, she wants to be just like Joss Whedon.

Chapter 6: Jamie Habermaas lives with her husband and their three sons in Southern Illinois. She spends her days working in a law firm and her evenings at home with her family. She enjoys living life by her personal motto of "Create Adventure. Live Inspired." sharing MS Awareness and living with positivity. You can read her blog at www.inspiredmess.com.

Chapter 7: Michael is a project manager for a commercial construction company in Kansas City. At one point in his varied career path, he was a locomotive engineer for Santa Fe Railroad, and still enjoys trains and the railroad industry. Michael's interests include travel, history, photography, writing and knowing God on a more intimate basis. To his misfortune, he has become adept at remodeling, and can't seem to get away from it! Michael lives in Lenexa, Kansas, a suburb of Kansas City, with his wife of many wonderful years, and has two amazing children whom he adores.

Chapter 8: Samurai is a pseudonym. I have been on my own since I was 16 and I am now a Husband (19yrs) and father of 3 in my mid 40's. Despite having dropped out of High School, I went on to become a 22 year veteran of the Army National Guard and a tier 3 technician for a government network as a contractor.

Chapter 9: Joy Wilson is the author of *Uncensored Prayer: The Spiritual Practice of Wrestling With God* (Civitas Press, 2011). She and her husband, Bud, are two life-long hippies. They live in Bartlett, TN, with six cats, two dogs, and a timber wolf hybrid. Joy is an Outlaw Preacher and an active participant in Kairos Prison Ministry. You can usually find her at home writing or intently reading history and mystery books. Contact Joy at joyleewilson@gmail.com.

Chapter 10: Crystal Clancy is a wife, mother of two, and Licensed Marriage and Family Therapist practicing in Apple Valley, MN. She is involved with Pregnancy and Postpartum Support MN (ppsupportmn.org), a non-profit that provides support and resources to parents struggling with adjusting to new parenting.

Acceptance

Chapter 11: Joy Bennett is a writer, mother of four, wife, book lover, follower of Jesus, bereaved parent, and asker of questions, in no particular order. Two of my children were born with serious congenital heart defects and between the two of them have had six open-heart surgeries. Despite the hardships, my husband and I are determined to beat the odds and enjoy a happy marriage.

Chapter 12: Travis Mamone is the co-host of the weekly podcast

Something Beautiful. He has written for such publications as *Relevant Magazine*, *The Upper Room*, and *Burnside Writers Collective*. He lives in Easton, MD, and blogs at www.travismamone.net.

Chapter 13: Misty Chaffins is a married, stay-at-home mom to two boys. Living life in small town WV, she shares some of it with readers on her blog at thechaffins.blogspot.com. You can usually find her being a chauffer for the children. Her hobbies include reading, making soap and generally pretending to be creative.

Chapter 14: Katie Alicea is a 30-year-old rambler, writer, giggler, and Jesus chaser. Born and raised in the rolling hills of West Virginia, she is a country girl at heart. She is married to the love of her life, Tony Alicea, and they live happily-ever-after in Southern Florida.

Chapter 15: Brooke Higinbotham is married to her husband of 19 years and has two children. She lives in Merrittstown, Pennsylvania. She is a stay-at-home mom. She is a vocal instructor, singer/songwriter and enjoys speaking to women's and marriage groups to encourage them to "run the course" and to not let life's speed bumps totally stop us in our tracks.

Chapter 16: Joanna Ross is married her high school sweetheart and now has a four children. She educates her children at home and enjoys sharing her love for learning with them. Some of the activities she enjoys are genealogy, local history, folklore, geology, and reading. In her spare time, she tries to find more room for all the books she has collected.

Chapter 17: Mary Balfoort has a B.A. in Psychology, and while she is not necessarily employed in the psychology field, she can reassure her mother that yes, she does use her degree. Mary is interested in photography, books, flower and veggie gardening, volunteering and relearning how to ride a bicycle. She works part-time for a local

GLBT center and has finally found a job that she absolutely loves. She lives in southwestern Michigan with her best friend/wife, five cats, and one 50lb dog who occasionally reports on the weather via Facebook.

Chapter 18: Robin Farr is a freelance writer and speaker. Her work appears in *Welcome to My World*, an ebook about working mothers in all their forms. She writes about her experience with postpartum depression at farewellstranger.com. Robin lives in Victoria, BC with her husband, son and their Wheaten Terrier. When she needs a break or some inspiration she finds a trail and goes for a run.

Chapter 19: Jake Kampe is an associate pastor of small groups living in League City, Texas where he also trains and mentors small group leaders. He is also a freelance writer, currently working on his first book, *Naked Theology: Daily Meditations on Christianity* and was most recently a contributing writer for *The Practice of Love: Real Stories of Living into God's Kingdom* (Civitas, 2011). He has been married to his wife Kelly for 19 years, and has three boys: Ian (13), Lucas (7) and four-legged son, Dexter (6). You can contact Jake at www.nakedtheologytalk.blogspot.com.

Chapter 20: Jody Johnson is the author of three self-published books of poetry on lulu.com: *Anam Cara, Poetry of the Soul* (2007), *Communion* (2008), and *Touchstones* (2009). She works as a county child protection social worker, and is the mother of four opinionated children.

Chapter 21: Kristin Tennant is a freelance writer for corporate clients and also writes about family, faith, struggle and redemption at Halfway to Normal (www.halfwaytonormal.com) and The Huffington Post. She and her husband and their blended family live in a Midwestern university town, where one of their favorite pastimes is cooking and sharing meals and conversation with friends.

Recovery

Chapter 22: Christina writes the blog "Welcome To The Laundromat". Christina also is the administrative assistant and event coordinator for Monvee. She enjoys traveling, Chicago sports, hosting dinner parties, and is a documentary junkie.

Chapter 23: Following Jesus has led Jeremy Myers into some dark places where people rarely experience love or grace of any kind: He works as a prison chaplain. When he is not in jail, he goes with his wife and three daughters to find others who feel abandoned by God in order to touch them with His love. Jeremy Myers writes at www.tillhecomes.org. He was most a contributing writer for *The Practice of Love: Real Stories of Living into God's Kingdom* (Civitas, 2011).

Chapter 24: Megg Joosten is an aspiring librarian, working as an office assistant. When she isn't filing and doing data entry, she loves to read, write, watch old TV shows long off the air, make jewelry and cuddle with her cats. She lives in Seattle with her husband, Geoff and two insane cats. You can read more of her writing at http://www.librarianhousewife.blogspot.com

Chapter 25: Chad Jones lives in Arizona with his wife, Lisa, and their two children. He works professionally in IT, blogs five days a week at http://randomlychad.com, and never thought he'd be sharing his depression story with anyone anywhere. It is his hope that in doing so, others are encouraged to know they are not alone—because there's power in shared story.

Chapter 26: Joe Sewell is a software engineer and author of the blog

Consider †his! at http://conthis.blogspot.com. Joe is also working on a book tentatively titled *The God-Sized Church: Finding Your Place in His Place*. Joe lives in West Melbourne, FL, with his wife, Joy, and their one foot-long Chihuahua.

Chapter 27: Dana McCoy is a pseudonym for the author.

Chapter 28: Kyla is a blogger and deep thinker with a heart for justice. After traveling (some of) the world, she chose to plant her feet in the ground, trying to learn what it means to be settled as well as free. Kyla spends her time training for half marathons and getting to know as many people as humanly possible.

Chapter 29: Chuck Larish is (once again) the director of the music technology program at Iowa Western Community College. In his spare time, he enjoys spending time with his family as well as songwriting and recording under the name Quad Mini Jasons at quadminijasons.charleslarish.com. He continues to run as regularly as his schedule will allow.

Post-Depression Reflections

Chapter 30: Melissa Binstock is the 22-year-old author of *Nourishment: Feeding My Starving Soul When My Mind and Body Betrayed Me* (Health Communications Inc., 2011), a memoir recounting her experiencing with living with psychological and neurological disorders. Melissa was honored for her book by Mental Health America and the Tourette's Syndrome Foundation. She is currently a junior majoring in psychology.

Chapter 31: Michael D. Russo is a four-time published Author including *Why Bankruptcy Rocks and Success is Over-Rated!* and *Bankruptcy Rocks Revisited*. He is launching an online television show called *Bankruptcy Rocks TV* designed to help new entrepreneurs avoid the dangers he experienced. Michael is a sought after radio guest and speaker. He lives with his wife and three children in Adelaide, Australia.

Chapter 32: In May 2010, Leigh Kramer intentionally uprooted her life in the Chicago suburbs by moving to Nashville in an effort to live more dependently on God. Trained as a medical social worker, she is pursuing her dream of writing. She is a contributor for The Well Written Woman and blogs at HopefulLeigh: www.leighkramer.com.

Chapter 33: Jen is a stay-at-home mom with an educational background in journalism. She worked as a newspaper reporter for several years and decided to leave her job when she and her husband realized that their son had developmental problems and would need therapy. He is their life's greatest joy, other than living for God. She still enjoys writing when she can and in her free time she likes to work on photography and scrapbooking.

Chapter 34: Melody Harrison Hanson lives in Madison, WI with her husband and four children. She can be found studying Biblical texts, sitting in the sunshine with coffee or a good book, taking endless photographs or writing. She is working on a collection of poetry titled: *Going Quietly Sane* and blogs at: www.logicandimagination.wordpress.com.

Chapter 35: Allison lives in Hopkinsville, Kentucky where she is married to Ray Carroll, author of "Fallen Pastor" Civitas Press (2012). They have three daughters. Allison works full time as a Medical Laboratory Technologist and she blogs at fallenpastorswife.wordpress.com.

Chapter 36: Jason Wright is a proud father and husband. He works as a trainer for medical records software and enjoys being around forests, food, football and family, but not necessarily at the same time. His blog can be found at TokenAtheist.com.

Chapter 37: Tamara Lunardo blogs about life and faith at TamaraOutLoud.com, occasionally with adult language, frequently with attempted humor, and hopefully with God's blessing. A part-time freelance editor and writer and full-time stay-at-home-mom and wife, she holds a BA in English and her five children, when they let her; she almost never holds her tongue.

A Call For Submissions

Not Afraid, Stories of Finding Significance

Not Afraid: Stories of Finding Significance is a Civitas Press community project that explores stories of people who have overcome fears and found their significance in the process.

We are looking for real, honest stories of people who have face their fears and come through with a greater sense of their value. We encourage you to let it all out on the page, and share in detail both the external circumstances and the internal conflicts that arise because of it. We are NOT looking for self-help essays on solutions, professional opinions, or agendas.

Project Information: http://civitaspress.com/not-afraid-stories-of-finding-significance/

The Practice of Love, Volume 2

The Practice Of Love, Volume 2 is a Civitas Press Community Project that continues to explore a remarkably simple idea. What would it look like to practice love? What would happen if we actively chose to engage a deep sense of love even in hard places? The possibilities include a love for God, a love for the self, a love for a neighbor, and even a love for an enemy. What emerges will inspire and challenge the reader to reconsider what it means to live out the practice of love in our lives.

Project Information: http://civitaspress.com/the-practice-of-love-volume-2/

About Civitas Press

Civitas Press is a boutique publishing firm specializing in inspiring and redemptive ideas. We specialize in a new and unique publishing model by partnering with inspiring writers who want to develop their voice, create a compelling presentation, and get the word out. We are creating a close-knit family network of writers that are working together to help each other develop a powerful platform.

Civitas Press can be found online at http://civitaspress.com

Twitter: civitaspress

Facebook: http://www.facebook.com/Civitas-Press

OTHER BOOKS BY CIVITAS PRESS

The Practice of Love: Real Stories of Living Into Kingdom of God, Edited by Jonathan Brink

This collection of stories explores a remarkably simple idea. What would it look like to practice love? What would happen if we actively chose to engage a deep sense of love even in hard places? The possibilities include a love for God, a love for the self, a love for a neighbor, and even a love for an enemy. What emerges will inspire and challenge the reader to reconsider what it means to live out the practice of love in our lives.

Retail: $15.99 | 294 Pages

Down We Go: Living Into the Wild Ways of Jesus by Kathy Escobar

Down We Go is a practitioner's guide for creating and cultivating missional community. It's based on the idea of living into the Beatitudes, and explores what it means to follow Jesus into the hard places of suffering, inequality, and injustice in order to cultivate, hope, beauty, justice, equality, generosity and healing.

Retail: $15.99 | 278 Pages

Uncensored Prayer: The Spiritual Practice of Wrestling With God by Joy Wilson

In a world searching for honesty and integrity, author Joy Wilson is leading the way by proposing a bold and daring approach to prayer. What would it look like to engage God in a wrestling match, and live to tell about it? In this bold and beautiful account of Uncensored Prayer, author Joy Wilson shares her insights and experiences of taking a radical risk with God. Joy's experience will both shock you and invite you into a radically deeper experience of spiritual communion with God, one that revolutionizes your prayer.

Retail: $13.99 | 234 Pages